Hope [UN]deferred

Finding the Light While in the Tunnel

———————

Brett and Michele Rezewski

Book Cover by Derrick Robbins

Edited by Elizabeth Rempel

Formatted by Brooke J. Losee

ISBN: 979-8-9882205-0-3
ISBN: 979-8-9882205-1-0 (ebook)

"Hope deferred makes the heart sick, but desire fulfilled is a tree of life."

—Proverbs 13:12

Since this is true, so is the opposite. Hope not deferred makes the heart healthy, and that hope can only be found one way!

Head over to **hopeundeferred.com** to receive a music playlist of songs that have helped the Rezewski family.

Dedication

This book is dedicated to my bride, Michele Rezewski. This book would not be in existence if it weren't for what she went through; what she continues to go through day in and day out. Her tenacity through it all has been inspiring. I am so thankful she remains with us. Michele, I hope to celebrate many more years with you. I love you, Michele.

I also want to dedicate this to our three boys: Conner, Easton and Kaiden. We are so blessed to call them our children, and we are thankful for their role in our story. Boys, God has amazing plans in store for you.

Additionally, I want to dedicate this book to Michele's parents, Dan and Connie. Through their selfless acts of service to our family, I've been able to maintain my employment and strive to live as "normal" a life as possible.

Brett and Michele Rezewski

Acknowledgments

I (Brett) want to thank my parents, Ed and Pam, for being an example to me of how you should act when adversity comes. As I watched them live out their stories, they inspired me with their perseverance. My dad keeps pushing through the pain of numerous knee surgeries, and my mom courageously fought through a battle with breast cancer. She was diagnosed in 2004, around the same time my grandpa died of pancreatic cancer, but she vowed to be completely done with her treatments by the time Michele and I got married. And she made it! My parents flew from Michigan to Spokane, Washington, and my mom was able to walk down the aisle at our wedding on July 16, 2005. Shortly after that, she walked in the three-day, 60 mile Susan G. Komen Race for the Cure.

Without our church family at Southwest Bible Church, things would have been much harder for us. Even before the stroke, they ministered to us in ways that were unimaginable. They put their faith into *action*. We are truly blessed to be around such an awesome "cloud of witnesses" (Hebrews 12:1).

I also want to thank Julie Cranford. I turned to my Hope Heals community for help when I wrote about our experiences at the camp. She came to the rescue and delivered. You'll find what she shared in chapter nine.

Brett and Michele Rezewski

Table of Contents

Brett and Michele Rezewski

Foreword

"We are honored to call the Rezewskis friends and fellow members of the Young Suffering Club and part of our beloved Hope Heals Camp Community. Their story has uniquely captured our hearts because it is heartbreakingly similar to our own. A young mom's life is nearly ended through an unexpected and catastrophic brain issue, with ongoing complications and disabilities. A husband perseveres and advocates with great commitment and love. A family is forever changed, but nonetheless seeks resilience in the new normal they never imagined living.

"And yet this unique story also captures every heart because we all want to know how to keep living and even find gratitude for the hardest parts of our lives. Our brains need stories of overcoming, so we might know our own stories can be ones of overcoming too. Brett and Michele's book and hard-won lessons learned remind us our most difficult challenges can also be our most powerful assignments in life.

"What a powerful guidebook you hold in your hands. May it be part of your own story of healing and help illuminate some of your darkest tunnels with the hope of Jesus."

—Katherine & Jay Wolf
Co-authors of HOPE HEALS & SUFFER STRONG

Brett and Michele Rezewski

Preface

You've heard those unbelievably inspirational stories—the ones movies are made of—in which it seems nothing can go right for the main character. They lose everything and find themselves in dire straits. Then, as the story progresses, good things start happening. They get the job they dreamed of as a kid that felt unattainable; they tap into their superhuman ability to win the championship game; they charm their childhood sweetheart after life's crazy twists and turns. Their lives turn out to be better than they were before they lost it all.

But what about the people who don't succeed, or those who fail to overcome? Do their stories not matter? Are they forgotten?

You've heard the cliché: "There is a light at the end of the tunnel." But what if the tunnel seems so long the light isn't visible? That tunnel might just feel like a black hole. Without a doubt, there are many people living in that tunnel, searching for the light, but not finding it.

I want to speak to those people. I want to speak to you. Let me encourage you; don't give up. Keep leaning in. Continue to persevere, especially through the hard things. Your character is becoming ironclad, and you *will* reap the benefits. I believe your purpose is on the other side of your suffering. I want you to know that even though it seems like there isn't a light at the end of the tunnel, it's there. It always has been, even though it hasn't been apparent. "Then Jesus again spoke to them, saying, 'I am the Light of the world; the one who follows Me will not walk in the darkness, but will have the Light of life,'" (John 8:12).

Dear friend, let me tell you, your story *matters*! I see you. My family sees you. You got this!

Introduction

Parts of this book were very hard for me to write. Quite often, writing brought me back to the moment it all happened; all the emotions I felt resurfaced as tears streamed down my cheek. However, those tears brought more healing to my heart. Writing this book has been therapeutic for me. The idea that our story can be used to help others through their own dark tunnels encourages me. That's why I was led to write.

Many parts of our story describe how God breathed His breath of life into us and gave us hope—[UN]deferred hope. On many occasions, the timing when parts of our story unfolded had to be very specific. If the timing differed at all, it might have had a drastic impact on the outcome. Minimizing the events to be merely coincidences would be inappropriate. We believe that God is sovereign. He has supreme power and authority over everything, including the hard things that happen in your life. Every detail is according to His plan. It's important to remember what the Bible says in Romans 8:28; "And we know that God causes all things to work together for good to those who are called according to His purpose." His promises are true. No matter what you are facing or will face, God will use it for good if you are called according to His purpose.

Parts of this book were written to help you understand what some people go through when they are in the care of others. Many don't have the support that Michele had and still has to this day. They don't have anyone to speak up for them. I often wonder what would have happened to Michele without the support of family and friends. The pain and suffering we have been through seemed overwhelming at the time, but by the grace of God, we remain firm in our belief that good things will come; God will keep His promise that all our suffering was and is for good.

As I wrote this book, there were parts of the story I learned from Michele that I had never heard before. I gained a new perspective as additional details were revealed. This book is filled with hills and valleys to help you understand and experience the emotional roller coaster we've been on.

What you read of our story has been pieced together from various sources. For example, I wasn't there when Michele became ill out of the blue, but I have heard the recording of the 911 call, as well as accounts from others. In this book, you will learn the full story as I did—one piece at a time.

By writing, I feel like I'm being obedient to God. He put it on my heart from the very beginning to share our story. He's given me a passion for writing, and it's a privilege to use my passion to inspire others.

I also recorded our story to speak to those who feel like all hope is lost. I want people to know that whatever they are going through has meaning; nothing is wasted. There isn't any suffering that isn't used by God. He has a purpose for it all.

I have shared this story with a great number of people, many of whom are my patients. I'm an X-ray technologist, and sometimes patients come into my exam room expecting to get a few simple X-rays, but by the time they leave, a half hour or more has passed. One example of that was a Korea and Vietnam veteran. I can't even remember how the conversation started. I shared with him how the *only* way we have been able to handle our situation is by leaning on the Lord; He's the hero of our story. My patient didn't know what it meant to have a relationship with the Lord. He learned that day. I printed out some verses from Romans – the "Romans Road" – and gave them to him. If you aren't familiar with these verses, you can find them in the epilogue.

As that patient left my exam room, he told me, "I have *hope* now." I will never forget that. Our story gave this man hope. A few months later, I had the opportunity to connect with him again. He told me that he looks at those verses I printed out for him every day. I could tell he was finally filled with *joy*. I could see it in his eyes, which were more vibrant than before. His mood appeared more cheerful as well.

Because we have a hard story to share and are passionate about it, people listen. Those who have gone through tough times know they aren't alone. When they share their story and I share ours, they know I get it. We get it! That's why I wrote this book. If our story can have an impact on people who hear it one-on-one, I have no doubt the same will happen with many, Lord willing.

As you read, I ask that you take notice of the timing of events as they happened. If the timing was any different, it could have had life-changing implications.

Brett and Michele Rezewski

CHAPTER 1

The Event that Changed Everything

My cell phone was buzzing in my pocket as I was finishing up taking X-rays on a patient. I did the right thing and ignored the call. Less than five minutes later, my phone buzzed again, while I was with the same patient. Usually when I get more than one consecutive phone call, something is going on at home that needs my attention. I quickly finished up with the patient, grabbed my phone, and saw Michele had called both times.

I returned the call as soon as I could. Surprisingly, Michele didn't answer; instead, it was Conner, our nine-year-old firstborn son. I'll never forget his words: "Dad, mom is not okay. You need to leave work IMMEDIATELY!" The next moment, I heard another voice on the phone that I wasn't expecting. It was our good friend, Shannon.

Shannon had been driving her daughter home from a birthday party and just *happened* to be at the right place at the right time. She doesn't live near us, but was on a street close to our home when she saw a fire truck make a turn heading in our direction. She had a strong feeling that she needed to follow, so she did. With every turn the fire truck made, she grew more worried that something had happened to my family. As the fire truck came to a stop in front of our home, her suspicion was confirmed; she witnessed the paramedics rush into my house. Conner was there to answer the door while on the phone with a 911 dispatcher.

Shannon told me the paramedics were taking Michele to the hospital. My heart sank. What was going on with Michele? She was only 35 years old – too young for something bad to happen, right? Thoughts continued to flood my head. What's going on with my wife? How am I going to handle working and taking care of our three kids? Automatically, I began to think the worst. It's amazing how so many fears can fill your brain in an instant.

The phone was passed to another person. This time, it was a deputy from the local sheriff's department. He asked me questions about Shannon to make sure it was okay for the kids to be in her care. Of course, it was. Shannon is a good friend, and I was thankful she was there, so I didn't have to worry about the kids. The deputy told me to go to the hospital in Beaverton, where they were taking my wife.

I was scared. As I hung up the phone, tears streamed down my face. I told my shift lead I needed to go, quickly gathered my things, and ran to the car.

The Diversion that Saved Her Life

My phone rang again. This time it was the paramedic. They called to inform me that Michele was being diverted to a hospital in Portland. They realized how severe Michele's injury was and that the Beaverton hospital wasn't equipped to handle her. Had they sent her there, she probably would have been airlifted to Portland. We were told that if Michele had arrived 15 to 20 minutes later, she would have died. I believe this diversion was providential. Driving at this time was probably dangerous for me. I was hysterical. Tears prevented me from focusing on the road. All I could think about was if Michele was going to be okay. And the baby... Michele was six weeks pregnant. Was the baby going to make it? *We already lost one baby several years earlier, please not another, Lord,* I prayed.

For some reason, my phone wasn't giving me good directions. It took me on the freeway, then off, then back on again. Speaking of not being in the right frame of mind to drive, I completely blew a solid red light. Only by God's grace were there not any other cars crossing. Otherwise, I may have joined Michele in the hospital as a patient—or worse.

I finally found the hospital, parked the car, and ran to the entrance. Cian, Shannon's husband, was there, so I wasn't alone.

The hospital staff directed me and Cian to a private room. I still had no idea what had happened to Michele. It felt like an eternity waiting for someone to tell me what was going on. I became frustrated and sought out answers myself; I left the room and went searching for someone, anyone wearing scrubs, that might know *something*. I'm sure I looked like a wreck as people passed me in the hallway, but I didn't care.

One of the staff members found me frantically roaming the halls, and I was directed back to the room. I was told somebody would come out shortly. SERIOUSLY!? I wanted to know *now*! I could feel the anger building inside me as if I were a human pressure cooker. My emotions were becoming incredibly difficult to control.

"The Worst News I Ever Heard"

A short while later, there was a knock at the door. Two gentlemen walked in. One was a chaplain; the other was an ER doctor. The words that came out of their mouths were, as Cian describes, "the worst news I ever heard." They told me that Michele was "really sick" and that her chances of survival were "grim." I learned that she experienced a spontaneous hemorrhagic stroke and was now being prepped for surgery. Based on a CT scan on her head, the ER doctor thought that Moyamoya disease could be the culprit. He then told me that his adopted sister had died from Moyamoya, even though she had been in great shape. In fact, she was lifting weights when a stroke killed her instantly.

Immediately after they broke the news, my knees became weak, and I collapsed to the floor. I had so many questions – questions for both the doctors and God. Was Michele going to make it through this? If she did make it, what would life be like for her? What was life going to be like for us? Did I do something to cause this to happen? Did Michele? Are we being disciplined because of some sin we committed? Why would God allow something like this to happen? We're *good* people, right?

Isn't it natural for people to ask questions like this? We wonder why bad things happen to good people, but here's God's perspective on "good" people: Romans 3:10-11 says, "As it is written, 'There is none righteous, not even one; there is none who understands; there is none who seeks for God.'" As far as questioning whether this happened as some sort of punishment, I'll attempt to answer that later on.

"You Need to Fight for Us"

The time had finally come for me to see her. A strange feeling came over me as I was led to her room. It was the most surreal experience I've ever had, like one of those "out of body" moments you hear about in movies.

Turning the corner into Michele's room, I found myself in a familiar scene; as an X-ray tech, I had been in many hospital rooms where the patient had coded (gone into cardiac arrest). The Code Team members each performed different tasks, but in harmony, like a magnificently choreographed Broadway production. What was foreign to me, however, was that my wife was the patient. She had wires all over her and a tube down her throat. The tube was her life support, which was the only source of oxygen for her seemingly lifeless body. The staff were prepping her for the fight of her life. I tried to take it all in. I went over to kiss her on the forehead, and as I did, I whispered in her ear, "Michele, don't give up! You need to fight for us!"

A couple of years after the stroke, Michele told me that even though she couldn't respond, she heard me say those words. She even recalled thinking, "Wait! What happened? Are the boys okay? What am I fighting for?" She wanted to yell, but couldn't open her mouth. Even when Michele was near death, she was thinking of our boys.

It didn't take long at all for the on-call neurosurgeon, Dr. David Antezana, to arrive. Right away, I could tell that Michele was in good hands. He reiterated the severity of the injury and informed me that time was of the essence. I stood by and watched as they ushered Michele to an operating room.

I Wasn't Alone

I met up with Cian again, and we were escorted to a waiting room. Once there, I started telling people about what had happened. I attempted to gather my composure to call my good friend, John, but as I explained what was going on, I broke down again. Within fifteen minutes of that phone call, people dropped what they were doing to come offer support; John notified our small group Bible study, and soon they, Pastor Scott, and other church family members arrived at the hospital. They formed a circle of chairs, so everyone could sit beside me in that waiting room. About 25 friends had come to be with me.

Pastor Scott initiated a time of prayer, and then he turned to Romans 8. This part of scripture has been my bedrock ever since. I believe he started in verse 26, saying, "In the same way, the Spirit also helps our weakness; for we do not know how to pray as we should, but the Spirit himself intercedes for us with groanings too deep for words." He was forced to pause because of an update from one of the staff members, but once they left, he picked up in verse 27 and continued.

Another interruption came shortly after. This time it was me. As I read along on my phone, I noticed a verse I had highlighted previously– verse 18. Pastor Scott encouraged me to read it out loud. I tried to gather my composure, took a breath, and let the words speak to my heart as they rolled off my tongue; "For I consider that the sufferings of this present time are not worthy to be compared with the glory that is to be revealed to us." Those words suddenly took on new meaning for me. I realized that the passages I studied previously were used to prepare me for this moment. Less than a month before the stroke, my church had wrapped up a detailed study on the book of James, where the men of Southwest Bible Church would gather in the foyer every Tuesday, sit in small groups, and dive into this amazing book.

"Consider it all joy, my brethren, when you encounter various trials, knowing that the testing of your faith produces endurance. And let endurance have its perfect result, so that you may be perfect and complete, lacking in nothing," (James 1:2-4).

OK, Lord, I hear you. But how am I supposed to be joyful at a time like this? Some people's faith gets shaken when trouble comes, and for many who don't believe in God, trials are another argument against the existence of a divine being. They say, "If there is a God, why did He allow this to happen?" We act as if we're entitled to only good things. Why are we thankful for the good but condemn the bad? How can there be one without the other? I've learned that having joy is a choice. Having joy during hardship, I believe, is only possible in the Lord. Having the *hope* that is *undeferred*, is only possible in the Lord.

There were multiple meetings throughout the night as the doctors and nurses came to give us updates on the surgery, and Pastor Scott proved to be a valuable resource. I gave him permission to accompany me to every meeting with the healthcare staff, mainly to be a second set of ears for conveying the message to everyone else. Pastor Scott stayed by my side, sitting forward in his chair and listening attentively to every word we were told. He was like a rock to me.

God is Moving in the Church

Pastor Scott didn't leave the hospital until after midnight, when he was relieved by Larry, an elder of the church. Pastor Scott still gave the sermon at 8:30 that next morning, though. As he waited for the service to start, he "rewrote" his talk in his head due to the impact of our experiences at the hospital the night before. He had planned to preach from Acts 16:19-40, but he didn't feel right just continuing where he left off the week prior.

Three years after the stroke, as I prepared to write this chapter, I watched that sermon again. I wasn't at the church when he preached that day; I was with Michele, where I needed to be. The first time I watched the sermon was later that week, when I gathered the family at home to watch the recording together. I got Conner's attention as the pastor called out his name. He spoke about how Conner dialed 911. Our nine-year-old son saved Michele's life.

Pastor Scott only focused on one verse from the section he was planning to teach, and that was Acts 16:25, which reads, "But about midnight Paul and Silas were praying and singing hymns of praise to God, and the prisoners were listening to them." It's important to understand the context of this verse to see how Pastor Scott related it to the night at the hospital, so here is Acts 16:22-24: "The crowd rose up together against them, and the chief magistrates tore their robes off them and proceeded to order them to be beaten with rods. When they had struck them with many blows, they threw them into the inner prison and fastened their feet in the stocks."

The next verse, 25, talks about Paul and Silas *singing*. I don't think it is normal for people to be singing after they were severely beaten with rods and thrown into "the inner prison." But they were filled with the Holy Spirit. They *chose* joy during their suffering. The other inmates knew of the situation, I'm sure; they had to know the Apostle Paul and why he was locked up with Silas. I can only imagine the impact those two disciples' singing had on their fellow prisoners.

So why would Pastor Scott compare this passage of scripture to what happened that fateful day? One reason could be because of their reaction to their situation, and my reaction to ours. The greatest common factor with both scenarios is the Lord, not us. I like a phrase one of our friends uses. She says, "Let Him increase, so that I may decrease." Then she'll include her equation: HE > i. People often ask me how I do it. My response is simple; it's not me, but the Lord who gives me strength. He gives me the strength to choose joy.

During the sermon, Pastor Scott spoke about not expecting an easy life just because you're a Christian. In fact, the Bible teaches that the opposite is true. Luke 9:23 says, "And He (Jesus) was saying to them all, 'If anyone wishes to come after Me, he must deny himself, and take up his cross daily and follow Me.'"

Jesus did. He took His cross. He knew He was going to be betrayed by people in His inner circle. He knew He was going to be falsely accused. He knew He was going to be beaten beyond recognition and nailed to a cross. He knew people were going to mock Him and spit on Him. Worst of all, He knew His Father was going to turn His back on Him because Jesus bore the sins of the world. God despises sin, and yet Jesus drank the cup of suffering. Why are we so hesitant to do the same? Paul says in Acts 14:22 that "Through many tribulations we must enter the kingdom of God." We aren't called to side-step trials; we are called to go *through* them. To keep pushing on, through that dark tunnel.

One other thing I want to highlight from Pastor Scott's sermon that day is the term *koinonia* (koy-now-nee-uh). This is a Greek word that means "partnership" or "fellowship." Pastor Scott witnessed koinonia in action that night as Michele was in surgery and the outcome was very much up in the air. He witnessed the partnership we have in the gospel as person after person came in, hugged me, and said, "There are no words," or "I don't know how to pray as I should." He exhorts later in the sermon, "If you don't know how to pray, just go to Romans 8 and read it out loud. Let that be your prayer."

Thankful for More Good Friends

Rich was another person I was incredibly thankful to have with me. He's an MD, and his expertise was helpful; I wanted him to be part of the meetings with the healthcare team. He accepted my invitation and joined me and Pastor Scott. Rich also agreed to talk with my supervisor at work and was able to share the news in medical terms. Over and over, a chilling word was used to describe Michele's prognosis. That word was "grim." I was told that the next 24 to 48 hours would tell us whether she would live or die. Then, I was told that if Michele survived, she would be "like a vegetable."

More Family Arrives

As soon as Ryan, Michele's younger brother, heard about what had happened, he and his wife Regina packed up their car and headed out, along with their newborn, Thea. Fortunately, they only live about three hours away from us. I know how difficult traveling with a newborn can be, so I'm thankful they made the effort to come to the hospital. It was good to see them, and it meant a lot to have their support. I was excited to see my niece for the first time too, although I wished it were under different circumstances. It was disappointing that Michele wasn't able to meet her at that point.

Remembering people's ages and birthdays is not one of my strengths, but I will always remember how old Thea is. I just think about how many years it's been since Michele's stroke. The Lord chose June 10, 2017, to be our demarcation line; the point in our lives where there was a clear separation between how things were before and after the stroke. From then on, we had a "new normal."

Soon after Ryan and Regina arrived with baby Thea, Michele's parents, Dan and Connie, touched down at the Portland Airport. They flew in from Spokane, Washington in *miraculous* fashion. At five p.m., they received a phone call from me informing that Michele was in the hospital. They were gathered around the table to eat dinner with their small Bible study group at the time. Once I found out she had a stroke, I phoned them again. They, along with their group, sprang into action. One person called and booked a flight, the ladies helped them grab some clothes and put away dinner, and a gentleman drove them to the airport. That gentleman was a deputy with the Spokane County Sheriff's Department; he made sure they got to the airport expeditiously. His efforts paid off as Dan and Connie were able to sit in the last two available seats on the last plane of the day. I believe God ordained those seats for them. Once they landed, a family friend met them at the airport and drove them to the hospital.

Steve, another close friend, waited for her parents and escorted them to the waiting room. Steve was a nurse at the hospital who was assigned to the same unit Michele was admitted into immediately following surgery. He wasn't supposed to be working that day, but he had traded with a coworker a few days before this incident. Because of what happened to Michele, his supervisor allowed him to be with me the rest of his shift. He was a huge support for me then, and remains so to this day. Steve is an awesome servant of the Lord.

The Damage

For perspective on how bad Michele's stroke was, here is some information; 200 milliliters (cc) of blood pooled on the right side of her brain following a ruptured artery. Dr. Antezana extracted 80 milliliters of blood through a "burr hole" that was drilled into her skull on the way to surgery, which was necessary to relieve pressure. Just picture an inflated balloon. What happens when you apply too much pressure? It bursts!

In the operating room, they pumped an additional 117 milliliters of blood into a bag. The amount of blood extracted from her brain alone was equivalent to almost seven fluid ounces. That pressure caused the midline section of her brain to be pushed 2.5 centimeters to the left.

Dr. Antezana started the operation by removing the right half of her skull. He knew going into the surgery that portions of her brain were already irreparable, so he then proceeded to remove most of her right temporal lobe and part of her frontal lobe. It is truly amazing that she is still with us. I was told by his physician assistant that if Dr. Antezana didn't have *hope* in her survival, he would've stopped the surgery early on. I believe that hope came from the Lord. I am so thankful we had a man of faith helping to preserve Michele's life.

Michele's outcome was still unknown after the surgery. We were told the next 24 to 48 hours were crucial. This whole time our boys had been at home with Shannon, so when Dr. Antezana came out to talk to me, I asked him what I should do about our children. I wanted to know if I should bring them in to see their mom and possibly say "bye." I will never forget his response. He said, "Jesus said, 'Let the little children come to Me!'" He used Matthew 19:14 to respond to my question.

The Boys Arrive

Upon my instruction, Shannon quickly gathered the boys and drove to the hospital. I met them at the elevator, gave them a big hug, and walked them towards our group in the waiting room. I could tell they were nervous after they saw how many people were with me. Imagine being in their shoes. You know that something just happened to mom. As you enter the hospital, you see a large group of people, and you know they are all here because of what happened to her. I can't imagine how overwhelmed they must have been. It had to have had an impact on them. Later, our middle son, Easton, drew a picture of his mom in her hospital bed with people gathered around her. He was well aware of what was going on, even at five years old.

After the surgery, Michele was sent to the Neuro Critical Care Unit (NCCU). We had been limited as to how many people could see her at a time, but they made an exception when the boys arrived. However, before I brought them in, I requested to see her by myself. I wanted to be able to prepare the boys as much as possible.

What I saw was heartbreaking. Both her eyes were swollen shut from the bleeding as if she had been punched in the face. A blue helmet was on her head to protect the rest of her brain after the skull was removed. She had lines coming out of her body everywhere, including a central line into her heart for medication. She also had a tube down her throat.

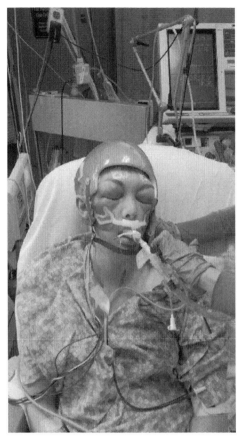

In addition to all that, it was evident that other parts of her body were affected from the nerve damage. Her whole body was tense (this is referred to as hypertonicity). Her head was fixed in a downward position and pulled towards her left shoulder; her left elbow was fully bent; her clenched left fist was pulled into her jaw; her right foot was fully extended and rotated inward, probably because the bleeding affected both sides of her brain due to the midline shift.

I took some time to gather myself before I went to bring the boys in. I had to figure out how to explain what they were going to see. But it didn't really matter. Nothing I could've said would have been enough.

When I returned to the waiting room, I brought the boys in close and gave them another hug. I asked them if they wanted to see mom. Conner and Easton wanted to go, but Kaiden, who was two, wasn't ready—he stayed behind. I ushered them in alongside Michele's mom, and they bore witness to the aftermath of the single event that changed the trajectory of our lives forever. We all stood in silence other than the audible sobs as we gazed at Michele in disbelief. After a time, the boys wanted to lean in to give her a hug, but didn't know how because of all the lines. They didn't want to hurt her anymore. I helped them at least get some contact with Michele. Because we didn't know if she was going to live or die, I wanted them to have some closure if she didn't make it.

On top of how the stroke affected her physically, we learned she might have other issues due to the extensive brain damage. The area of her brain that was damaged controls perception, decision-making, language, and consciousness. It's basically where the human experience lives. The temporal lobe, which is where the majority of the damage took place, also controls auditory memories, reactions to music, fear, sense of identity, visual memories, some hearing and speech, and facial recognition. That last one was big for me; we didn't know if she would recognize us. I couldn't imagine her not knowing who I was, or the boys, or anyone for that matter. Thankfully, most of those potential symptoms didn't end up being an issue. She does still have some memory loss, but nothing significant.

The stroke also affected Michele's ability to swallow. She was deemed NPO (nothing per oral), so a feeding tube was placed in her nose. Later, a more permanent feeding tube was inserted directly into her stomach. Still, because of her inability to swallow, saliva began pooling in her mouth and required constant suction to prevent it from getting into her lungs. Despite our efforts to keep her system clear, a later chest X-ray showed consolidation in her lungs, which meant she had developed pneumonia. Could anything else go wrong?

The Decision that Changed Everything

It was only a couple of days after Michele's stroke that I resolved I wouldn't let this shape my family negatively. That conscious decision has given me the foundation to move forward and lead my family. I believe it was one of the most important decisions of my life: to show up for my loved ones in the best way I possibly can, while relying on the Lord for strength.

There is no doubt in my mind that God prepared me for this time. Even in my grief, I knew that how I responded to the situation could have a significant impact on our boys' lives. He gave me the grace and the strength to have that clarity early on. If I'd let anger get in the way, bitterness and resentment could have crept in. The boys could have developed a poor relationship with God, or no relationship at all. It could have negatively impacted their future relationships, among many other things.

As I said earlier, I believe God prepared me for Michele's stroke. It wasn't by chance that we found Southwest Bible Church. It was all according to His plan. Also, it wasn't by chance that the book we studied just before the stroke was James. God led me to a smaller, more intimate group of men that met at a coffee shop Friday mornings at 6 a.m. Each week, we went through a chapter of the

Bible and dissected it. It was helpful to hear scripture read out loud as we went around the circle. After reading, the men offered insights as to what spoke to them from the passage. I felt the nuggets the men shared were solid; they are all sound thinkers, and most importantly, they love the Lord.

When I first started going to the meetings, I was intimidated by how intellectual the conversation sounded. But, it inspired me to grow. Soon I started adding to the discussion. I still mostly listened, but maybe once a week God would give me a solid "one-liner" to contribute.

In addition to the biblical lessons we learned each week, there was accountability. We prayed for one another. We felt comfortable bringing our struggles to the group and then to the Lord together. We all desired to be godly leaders for our families and to honor Him. That group was the first place I was really challenged to dive deeper into my relationship with the Lord. I knew prior to that, I was just "going through the motions."

Trying to Take Back Some "Normalcy"

What is normal? Is your life normal? Our life sure isn't. Does "normal" even exist? Or is it an illusion that causes people to "chase after the wind", constantly searching for that one thing that will give them a warm and fuzzy feeling?

Before the stroke, we thought we lived a relatively normal life. I worked Monday through Friday with the evenings off. Michele cooked dinner and we ate as a family. We shared the responsibility of raising the kids and cleaning the house, just like most couples. But we took our livelihood for granted. The stroke rocked our world. The small things of life became more noticeable, and we were thankful for each small victory Michele had.

I fought to regain some sense of normalcy. Just days after the stroke, I arranged for someone to be at the hospital, so I could be home with the boys. But it wasn't normal at all. Michele's future was still largely unknown. The house felt empty; it didn't even feel right to sleep in my own bed. Most nights, I fell asleep next to one of the boys or on the couch.

I'm not usually one to get anxious or feel stressed, but it hit me hard one night while I was alone with the kids. I didn't realize how shot my nerves were until I snapped. Easton's never-ending questions finally got to me. You know how five-year-olds are; their brains are always going and wanting to learn. Also, they know how to push your buttons. If I had a red button that would launch a nuclear strike, Easton pushed it that day. I lost my temper. I yelled at him and stormed off. But God used the next moment to completely change my heart. Realizing what I had just done, I collapsed to the floor in hysteria. Easton came over to me, got down on the floor, and gave me a hug. He started crying as well, and said, "Dad, it's okay." Man, the waterworks started flowing. Can you believe it? A five-year-old having enough maturity to realize the situation and offer encouragement to *me*. I didn't deserve it, but God used Easton to show me grace. I am so thankful we serve *that* kind of God.

Brett and Michele Rezewski

CHAPTER 2

Progress

You've heard the cliché, "one day at a time." Well, we truly learned how to take it one day at a time. It was more like one minute at a time. We still didn't know what Michele's future would look like.

Slowly, she started to make progress. Two days after the stroke, we had our first response from her; while the nurses were doing their regular checks, she responded to commands! At first, it was, "Lift two fingers." She lifted two fingers. "Wiggle your toes." She wiggled her toes. "Squeeze my hand." She squeezed their hand. This was VERY good news. There is always the possibility that people who have experienced serious brain trauma will become brain-dead, but because Michele responded to commands, we found *hope* that she was going to be okay. Only time would tell what she would get back, though. We were still told to prepare for the worst.

At the time, I knew Michele couldn't communicate with us, but I was sure she could hear us. I wanted to give her as much encouragement as possible, so at home I recorded Conner reading some scripture passages. I also captured Easton saying encouraging words and some of Kaiden's babble. When I played those recordings for Michele, I knew she heard them because her heart rate would increase. It's probably safe to say she was excited to hear her boys. Unfortunately, her increased heart rate meant that I had to stop playing the recordings, since that could raise her internal temperature and cause further brain damage. I'm sure she enjoyed listening while she could.

It's amazing how tragedy can change your perspective. We learned to appreciate all the little things in life that we so often took for granted. For instance, just watching Michele lift two fingers gave us so much joy! I challenge you to spend some time reflecting on what you have and what you're able to do. Allow this to give you an *attitude of gratitude*.

Friends in High Places

On top of having a friend who was a nurse in the same unit where Michele was receiving care, an elder of our church, Gary, was a highly respected cardiac surgeon. I first met him in the hospital after Michele was admitted, and it felt like having him on our side gave us instant access to whatever Michele needed. He funneled requests to the leaders on our support team, and they listened to him. He also sat with Michele whenever possible at night and prayed over her. Prayer was not lacking for my beautiful wife.

Michele's lead physical therapist was amazing and quickly became loved by the whole family. Just one day after the stroke, she had Michele on her feet! That was no small task. Pastor Scott came to visit that day and just happened to walk in as we were working to get Michele out of bed. It took two therapists, her nurse, and me to accomplish the feat. There were lots of wires and lines that we had to maneuver around, and she was still intubated.

Getting Michele on her feet as quickly as possible was vital. Standing sent a signal to her brain that told her this was the correct position to be in, rather than lying in bed. While she was upright, we moved around all the equipment and transferred her to a reclining chair. It was important to get her sitting up at least once a day. This was all part of the healing process—to start the "rewiring" of her brain.

Leading the Lord's Army

Within the first week, I called a meeting to have all the elders of the church come to pray over her. Gathering all the men at one time was a difficult undertaking, but they all showed up. First we prayed out in the waiting room. Then, I went back to her room by myself to let her nurse know everyone was there. Initially, only two or three people were supposed to visit her at a time because her condition was so volatile, but they made an exception under one condition: if her heart rate increased, everyone would leave. Before we entered the room, we prayed that her heart rate would stay consistent.

As I marched down the hall with at least ten elders behind me, I felt like we were going to war. I led the army, and our adversary was the devil. We all joined in a circle around Michele and prayed. Instead of her heart rate increasing, it went down! I believe the Holy Spirit calmed her. Each man took their turn speaking life over

Michele and praying to the one who can "sympathize with our weaknesses" (Hebrews 4:15). I continuously looked at her monitor and watched her heart rate, and when I saw the rhythm decrease, I knew Satan was losing.

I could only imagine what the people outside the room – the doctors, nurses, and others who were there with loved ones – would have thought seeing all the men gathered in a circle of prayer, and what the impact the sight might have had on them. Yes, God had a reason for Michele's stroke, and He still does. What Michele went through and lives with every day is hard, but I again consider Romans 8:18; "For I consider that the sufferings of this present time are not worthy to be compared with the glory that is to be revealed to us."

Missed Diagnosis

We quickly became accustomed to different healthcare workers coming in throughout the day. There were internal medicine doctors, nurses, nursing assistants, respiratory therapists, occupational therapists, speech therapists, social workers, chaplains, the IV team, neurologists, radiologists, X-ray techs – the list goes on. It was very helpful that I was a healthcare worker myself. As a healthcare worker, I understood the message about what the medical team was conveying about the severity of the stroke and her future. With this understanding, I was also able to communicate to family and friends what was going on, and my background gave me an idea of what to expect. I had become comfortable talking with doctors, having worked with them every day. One other advantage was knowing the doctors worked for *us*. Having this mindset was crucial as Michele advanced through the labyrinth of care during her six months away from home. Knowing that they worked for us meant that we could request someone new if we didn't feel Michele was getting the care she needed.

Michele was released from the NCCU within two weeks and was transferred up to the ward. We knew Michele wouldn't be at this hospital much longer, since it was out of our insurance network. Once she was transferred to the ward, the insurance company felt they could handle her care at their own facility. While we were thankful for Michele's progress, her leaving the NCCU was bittersweet. We knew where her next destination would be, and I had significant trust issues with them.

The Moyamoya disease could have been caught and corrected prior to the stroke that almost killed her. Michele had been complaining of headaches most of her life. Over the 12 years we were married, she had complained about headaches many times, and all that had been done was a CT scan of her sinuses. When we became enrolled with our insurance company, her providers never requested her old medical records. At every appointment Michele had where her headaches were the issue, she would mention that her paternal grandmother had died of what we believed was a brain aneurysm when she was 50, but because an autopsy wasn't performed, we weren't sure. We learned that Moyamoya disease is hereditary, and it's predominant in Asian women. Her grandma was full Japanese, which makes Michele one-quarter Japanese. It's possible her grandma had and was killed by Moyamoya.

My trust issues with our healthcare network originated from a comment I read days after the stroke. Because of Michele's history with headaches, I had wanted to dive into her medical records to see what was discussed at her appointments. Here is one comment from a doctor's note dated one and a half years *before* the stroke:

Headaches

Intermittent right sided sharp, intense, well localized pain that will last 1 minute or so

Occasionally will recur

Stops her in her tracks

At that appointment, Michele was diagnosed with anxiety and placed on an antidepressant. She was told that she's a busy mom and not to worry. If the doctors had ordered an MRI, the Moyamoya disease could have been caught and corrected with a bypass surgery. This doctor worked for the same company that had requested Michele once she was discharged from the NCCU.

Another golden opportunity where her condition could have been discovered was when Michele had sporadic fainting episodes. One of those had caused her to fall, and we had sought answers after that. It was thought that the fainting was due to heart issues. She had an EKG study and was instructed to wear a heart monitor, and both returned normal results. After that, nothing else was done.

Aside from the care itself, we also weren't looking forward to the transfer because of the hospital's location. We lived in Beaverton, and the hospital was about a forty-five-minute drive from our home on a good day. That increased our travel time by at least twenty-five minutes each way. It might not sound like a long time, but when you do it every day, it adds up. We wanted to be with her every day to make sure she was getting taken care of and because we didn't want her to be alone. Between Michele's parents, friends from church, and me, somebody was with Michele nearly all day, every day. I'm incredibly thankful we had so much support. It was sad to hear that we were the exception; so many people spend their hospital stays alone, without a loved one to help with their care.

Finding My Voice

We knew right away that the culture was different at the second hospital. In the first one, they used "baby" when talking about our baby, but in the second, our baby was called a "fetus." In addition to this, instead of the life-giving words spoken at the first, words of gloom were used. The hospitalist on staff at that time told us that Michele would never be able to open her right eye because the bleed pinched off one of her optic nerves. Another doctor, the neurologist, told us that she would never be able to eat again because the bleed pinched off her brain stem, which is where the signal to swallow comes from. Both doctors spoke these words to me as if Michele wasn't in the room, which upset me and raised my guard even more.

It was during this time that I found my voice. I needed to speak up for her. She couldn't do it. Our child couldn't do it. I used my occupation towards my advantage; but what about those who aren't in healthcare? Because I work with doctors and talk with them every day, I'm not intimidated by a few extra letters placed in front of their name, and fortunately for Michele, she had a team of family and friends who were all in agreement. But how many don't have that? How many people are intimidated by doctors and go along with things they feel may not be in their best interest? Just to be clear, I have the utmost respect for healthcare providers, but some should not be in the business of caring for people.

Shortly after the transfer, I called a meeting with the key players in Michele's care. I wanted to set the tone and to let them know that we were there as Michele's voice. Here are some key items I brought up at that meeting; the following are direct quotes from the notes I took to prepare:

- Please plan and deliver care for Michele the way you would do for your family.
- What's inside her uterus is a baby, not a fetus. Please do not refer to my son or daughter as a fetus.
- Whether the baby makes it or not, God has a plan for that child!
  Her blood pressure was controlled better at the first hospital. (It was and is important to regulate her blood pressure because of the Moyamoya disease.)

Her pain seemed to be managed better at the other hospital. (She was in a lot of pain from the surgery.) Why isn't she being pushed more for PT (We knew the importance of Michele getting on her feet and being transferred to the chair. But many times, days had gone by when this didn't happen.)

Another topic we discussed pertained to the future operations she would need. Half of Michele's skull was being kept in the freezer inside a "bone bag." She needed to heal more and the swelling from her brain had to be completely gone before surgeons could rejoin it with the other part of her skull. We also needed to discuss when the left side of her brain could be corrected. Because the Moyamoya disease affected both sides of the brain, there was a chance she could have a stroke on the left side as well. We asked the neurosurgeon how many bypass surgeries he had done to correct Moyamoya. His response was, "None." They recommended Michele have the surgery at a hospital in San Francisco that was still within their network. Thankfully, we decided against that since we knew of a local Moyamoya expert who had done many of the bypass surgeries we needed.

I believe it was providential that Michele was initially diverted away from the Beaverton hospital and to the one in Portland for many reasons, but the main one being that that is where we met Dr. Vivek Deshmukh. He was starting the process of making his office one of the few Moyamoya centers in America able to perform the bypass surgery. Dr. Deshmukh is not only an amazing neurosurgeon, but he has great bedside manner as well, and it's hard to find a doctor with both skill sets.

Dr. Deshmukh wasn't the surgeon who operated on Michele the day of the stroke, but he became one of our greatest allies in the subsequent days. He checked on Michele and the family regularly. Immediately following the stroke, he had a hunch Moyamoya disease was the culprit, and he performed a cerebral angiogram to verify. After the two weeks we spent working with him, we were convinced that he was the one we wanted to have perform Michele's surgery to correct the arteriovenous malformation (AVM).

While Michele was a patient at the second hospital, we often spoke up. The physical and occupational therapy she received there was nothing like at the first. It was hard to settle for the new care she was getting when we already knew what good therapy looked like. We often inquired about why Michele wasn't getting out of bed; we wondered why she wasn't being pushed at all. It was also difficult with the constant changing of doctors that were caring for her. We would get used to one after a couple of days, and then they would rotate. Each new doctor brought new ideas – some good, some not so good, and some terrible.

Finding the Silver Lining

To be clear, the care she received wasn't all bad. Some of Michele's nurses were believers, which brought us encouragement. We were told some nurses prayed over her and read her scripture. On a couple of occasions, I heard songs by MercyMe coming from Michele's room; a nurse played it on her cell phone, so Michele could listen. That made my heart happy. It was exciting for me to hear that she was getting prayed over even while we weren't there. Prayer was, and still is, something we covet. Never underestimate the power of prayer.

Many times, as I sat next to Michele, I found myself reading the Bible; I needed the encouragement. God spoke to me often as I dug into His Word. I also had plenty of time to connect with friends on Facebook. I treated it as if it were a diary, and I received additional encouragement from people's comments. As I went back and read some old Facebook posts, I was reminded of one of my prayers. I had spent a lot of time in the Psalms, and in the post I had quoted Psalms 25:4-6; "Make me know Your ways, O Lord; teach me Your paths. Lead me in Your truth and teach me, for You are the God of my salvation; for You I wait all the day."

I talked with her nurses often. I shared about our family, our faith, and about how we were coping with the current tragedy. I wrote Bible verses on the whiteboard in the room. One of the rooms she was assigned to had a wall covered in mirrors. On that wall, I wrote Isaiah 40:28-31. That reads:

Do you not know, have you not heard?
The Everlasting God, the LORD, the Creator of the ends of the earth
does not become weary or tired.
His understanding is inscrutable.

He gives strength to the weary,

and to him who lacks might, He increases power.

Though youths grow weary and tired, and

vigorous young men stumble badly, yet those

who wait for the LORD

will gain new strength; they will mount up

with wings like eagles, they will run and not

get tired, they will walk and not become

weary.

It's exciting to think about how many people heard the gospel while Michele was away from home. Some might have heard it for the first time. Some reading this book might be hearing it for the first time. Three days after the stroke, I wrote a group text message to my close friends that read, "There are at least two good things that

I want to have happen through this. 1) More people coming to Jesus. 2) Being able to encourage and strengthen others in their faith, which is already happening." Early on, a deep seed was planted in my heart, a seed which spoke to me, telling me that the suffering we endured ought not to be wasted. As I write this book, that text is being carried out. I have no idea who will read these words, but I write in faith, *knowing* that they will reach the people who need them. This isn't just our story. This is God's story, and He will put it in front of those who need to hear it.

CHAPTER 3

Signing My Life Away

How many times have I signed my name before without even thinking about it? This time was different. This time, there was a life hanging in the balance. A precious life. It was someone who couldn't weigh in on this decision—this one decision with huge implications. This person couldn't speak up to say, "No. Wait!" This person had no idea what was coming next.

I found myself staring at a piece of paper with an "X" telling me where to sign, with the pen right beside it. The doctor had left me alone after describing, in detail, what the next steps for the procedure were. The moment he was gone, I lost all composure. I was practically convulsing; the emotional outbursts were bad. Through the tears, I stared at the table in front of me, knowing what I needed to do. I glanced between the piece of paper and pen, and even though it was only a couple of minutes, it felt like an eternity. I'm sure everyone who walked by the closed door heard every sob. Every heartbreaking, gut-wrenching sob. So many thoughts entered my head; I asked God why this had happened to Michele. I asked Him why I was put in a place where I had to decide whether to end the pregnancy. This could've been the baby girl we had hoped and prayed for.

I barely mustered the strength to pick up the pen, let alone write my name with it. Nonetheless, I took some deep breaths, fought back the tears, and reluctantly held the pen in hand while shaking uncontrollably. I knew it was time for the doctors to take my wife back to the operating room; they were just waiting on my signature. I knew what I needed to do. I'd prayed about it. I'd sought counsel from the church. I'd discussed it with Michele's parents. We were all in agreement that this was the right decision, but actually following through with it seemed unbearable.

Tears clouded my vision. I wiped them away, braced myself, and signed the document. There. It was done. I had just signed part of my life away. I tried to calm down; I had felt peace about the decision before being brought into the room, but where was that peace now? I sure needed it. I remembered the conversations I'd had with Tom and Gary, two members of the church that I highly respected. I remembered talking with Michele's parents, as well as my own. We were a team; what happened to one of us happened to us all.

When the doctor came back into the room, I broke down again. They were ready to take my wife back to terminate the pregnancy. All the doctors unanimously agreed that this was the best thing to do; they said that if we kept the baby, there was at least a 33 percent chance that Michele would have another stroke, and that the next one might take her home to be with the Lord. I wanted to give our three boys the best chance of growing up with their mom, and I didn't want to lose my wife. We were told that if we didn't abort our child, there was a good chance we would lose them both.

I left the room and stood with Michele's parents as we watched the staff push her stretcher towards the OR. Our sorrow came to a climax when she disappeared behind the restricted entry doors. I remember seeing the faces of the staff as they continued down the hall, glancing back at us. It was evident they shared in our grief; their faces were somber and their heads were down. This was hard on them, too. It seemed to me like they were moving in slow motion. Nobody felt any urgency to get this procedure underway. But this was just a part of their job.

Seeking Counsel: The Wise Thing to Do

Gary is a cardiac surgeon and fellow church member who gained our trust very quickly as he ministered to Michele and our family. During this pivotal time, he shared some decisions he had needed to make during his career that made the difference between life and death for his patients. He said that sometimes all options were exhausted, and he had to be the one to tell their families that he had tried everything.

Prior to signing that document to have our baby aborted, I talked with Gary about the impending decision. His words helped me find peace. He said, "God allowed Michele's injury to be so bad that the decision was already made for you." In other words, because of the severity of her injury, we knew that God had other plans for our baby. Even with something as hard as this, "God causes all things to work together for good to those who love God, to those who are called according to His purpose," (Romans 8:28). I believe in His promises, and that is a promise I stand on.

I also spoke with Tom, another church member. His words brought me peace as well. He said, "God, the Father, allowed His son to die so that we may live." Similarly, I was allowing our child to die so that Michele may live. The night I heard those words, I shared them with her parents, and they comforted us all. We agreed that ending the pregnancy was the right thing to do, even if the sanctity of life is a value we hold dear.

I wish I could have included Michele in the discussion. Her not being able to weigh in made it harder to come to terms with the decision. It was her body, her pregnancy; but she couldn't communicate yet. She wasn't fully aware of anything that was going on.

We had found out she was pregnant only a week before the stroke, and we were hoping for a girl. She was only six weeks along then, so it was too early for the baby to survive outside the womb. What if that was our daughter, though? Michele had always wanted a girl, and her intuition told her it was. But now we'll never know. What's even harder for us to grasp is that we'll never be able to have another baby; one of her doctors told me that she should not get pregnant again because of the Moyamoya disease and her history of stroke.

Following the procedure, I wasn't allowed to tell Michele what had happened. Everyone, including the family and staff, agreed that it wasn't the right time for her to know; we worried that she wouldn't handle it well emotionally, and that it would cause her to take a major turn for the worse. Withholding that information was incredibly difficult. I had to force myself to act like everything was okay. Looking back, I'm not sure if we made the correct decision, but at the time it seemed appropriate. Hindsight is always 20/20, right? We did tell her eventually, and honestly, I'm not sure if she even remembered being pregnant. Up until the news broke to her about terminating the pregnancy, she had never asked about the baby.

Why Did That Happen?

At the time of writing this, five years have passed since we parted with the child. Five years have passed since we parted with the idea of ever having another child again. Still, we can't help but wonder why that happened. There are some things in life that we'll never have the answers for.

When painful things happen, you are left with a decision to make; you can blame God, which usually leads to a life of bitterness and resentment, or you can accept the situation and trust that He has a plan for everything. Especially the hard things. With my decision to trust in God, I can know that He had other plans for that child. Those plans didn't involve the baby taking its first breath, but God can use our baby for good even still. He can use your story for good as well, even if it doesn't make any sense from our perspective.

Life Goes On, but Does It Need to Happen So Fast?

Do you ever wish that life would slow down? Have you felt like you're living every day in the fast lane, or that you don't have control? Days and weeks seem like a blur, and all you want to do is take a minute and just *be*. If you answered "yes" to those questions, I get it. My family gets it. Life goes on, because it must. Sometimes you just need to "roll with the punches," as they say.

Before the stroke, we made plans for the summer like most families do, and the kids had been looking forward to those activities for a while. It was going to be our second summer attending Family Camp at Trout Creek Bible Camp in Corbett, Oregon. I really didn't want to go, though; I wanted to stay with Michele. But, I knew the kids deserved to get away from all the craziness for a bit, and I knew Michele would be well looked after. Her parents were very diligent about making sure there was somebody with her at all times, and plus, some friends of hers had come to visit from out of town. So, after some consideration, the boys and I packed our bags and left. It was good to get away for a few days to be able to think, be around friends that loved us, and spend some quality time with the kids.

Family Camp with the Boys

Trout Creek Bible Camp is an amazing place. There are tons of activities; zip lines, archery, go-karts, paintball, canoes, mountain bikes, BB guns, basketball, carpetball, and many others. We were served food and waited on by the youth staff. The Lord knew what I needed; He always knows. On top of all that, everyone was excited about the parade and fireworks; the Fourth of July was coming up, and Trout Creek never disappoints with their firework show. While we were at camp, I knew I needed to tell the boys about the baby. I was thankful some friends from our area were there with us and agreed to watch two kids at a time, so I could be alone with the third. It was then that I told them the hard news. I didn't let them in on how the baby died, I just told them we had lost it; they didn't need to know all the details. Conner isn't usually one to express a lot of emotion, but I could tell it was like a punch in the gut for him. Easton was also sad; I could see it on his face. He had really wanted another brother or a sister. Kaiden was only two at the time, so he didn't really understand the situation.

Family Camp was just what we needed. I'm glad family and friends encouraged me to take the boys, even though everything inside me wanted to stay with Michele. It was good to have time to think and put things into perspective. I woke up early each day to read the Bible and pray. It's amazing how you can read some verses over and over without putting much thought into them. Then, you read those same verses after adversity strikes, and you find new meaning; you realize the power of scripture.

On the way back home, we and two other families from the camp stopped at the hospital to see Michele. We are so blessed to have such loving friends. For having so many kids in one small room, it actually wasn't too crazy. There were nine kids and five adults altogether, not including Michele, but thankfully, her room was large enough to accommodate us all. Together, we sang praise songs and gathered in prayer, and even the kids joined in. Despite how many transitions Michele had during her six months in hospitals, skilled rehab facilities, and acute therapy institutions, she somehow always had her own room. That was such a blessing.

Our Anniversary

A couple of weeks after Family Camp was our 12th wedding anniversary. I planned to have the kids stay with their grandparents for the night, so I could spend that time at the hospital with Michele. A new season of her favorite show, NCIS, was on Netflix, and I was excited to watch it with her.

It is common for people with traumatic brain injuries, especially as bad as hers, to have days that are worse than others. Unfortunately, that day was one of those days. It didn't go as planned. She wasn't fully aware of what was going on, and she slept a lot. I knew that was normal, and she needed rest for her brain to heal, but it was still a bit frustrating.

I don't usually journal, but I did for a while after the stroke to document milestones. A good friend, Toby, gave me a journal, and I'm so glad he did; if it weren't for those entries, I might have forgotten key details. Here is one from July 16, 2017:

Today is our 12th wedding anniversary. As I sit with her tonight, I am hurting. This isn't how this night was supposed to be. We had plans to spend the night at a Bed & Breakfast in Newberg. Instead, she is in her hospital bed, and I'm in the reclining chair next to her. I don't understand at all why this had to happen to her. I just wish He would heal her already. I do know that God has a plan for good things to come because of this. It may be awhile before we are able to see what they are...or we may never see those things, this side of heaven. But I do trust Him and His promises never fail.

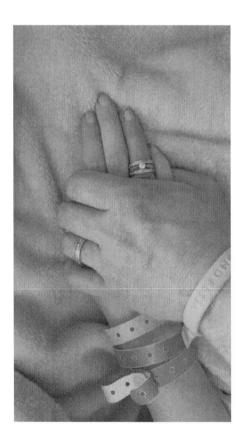

Baby Steps

It was exciting to see Michele progress in her recovery; there was a time in which we weren't sure if "recovery" and "Michele" were words we would say in the same sentence. Unfortunately, though, she still couldn't communicate. We knew she was in pain, but she couldn't tell us where. Then, Michele's brother, Ryan, had a great idea. During one of his visits with the family, he brought in a small white board with dry-erase markers so she could communicate by writing. He wasn't sure if it would work, but he felt it was worth a shot. I'm so glad that he did. Michele took the marker, we held the board, and she started writing a mile a minute. The first thing she wrote was, "Leg hurting." We showed that to her nurse, and the nurse passed it along to her doctor. They were worried that it could be a blood clot. It's common for people to get blood clots in their legs when they lay in hospital beds for so long. That's why they have cuffs around their legs that constantly squeeze and release; this promotes blood flow and keeps it from remaining stagnant. Because of what Michele had written on the white board, an ultrasound was performed. Thankfully, no blood clots were found.

Visits with Michele were quite different once she could finally share what was on her mind. This made the time we spent with her go by quickly. She gave us directions about things she needed, and we would jump to try to help her.

There were talks about Michele getting discharged and moving to a Skilled Nursing Facility (SNF), but a couple of things needed to happen before that could come to pass: the other half of her skull needed to be reattached, and we needed to tell her about the baby.

Prepping for surgery usually brings anxiety. While there was some of that when they took her back to get her skull replaced, we were also excited. We felt like Michele was progressing with her recovery, and getting her skull put back together was one more thing that could be crossed off the list. The surgeon placed metal plates, screws, and staples in her head to hold the two pieces of bone together while it healed. The scar that runs down the middle of her head still brings back memories and reminds me of all the suffering we've endured.

Don't we all have "scars" from our past? Whether they are physical or emotional, they all serve a purpose; none of them are wasted. It's those scars that make us who we are. We have a choice on how we view and respond to them. We can either choose to grow bitter or use them to help us grow. It's that choice that becomes our defining moment. If you are suffering, I encourage you to continue through that long, dark tunnel that may seem to never end. Continue the journey, my friend. God placed you there for a reason; lean into it.

Telling Michele about the loss of our baby was inevitable, but very challenging to confess. The same doctor who told me we shouldn't get pregnant anymore volunteered to make the task as easy for me as possible. She asked if I wanted her to go in with me to break the news. I thought that was a good idea. She approached the topic from a medical perspective and with the sanctity of Michele's life in mind. She basically took the burden off my shoulders. Yet, it didn't make it any easier; I was still crushed. However, Michele appeared emotionless, when we broke the news. Later on, Michele had shared that, "I think I knew all along that the baby was gone, but I couldn't voice it. I just wanted to ask…but I couldn't."

After the doctor left, I stayed with Michele. I wanted to make sure she was okay. As far as I could tell, she was, but I'm sure that there were many emotions she couldn't release beneath the surface. I was worried anger was one of them; anger towards God, and me, for taking the baby away from her. I did my best to be available if she had any questions. Since she had just found out, and I had been grieving for a while already, I kept in mind that we were in different phases of processing.

To this day, she still struggles with the decision I made. She wonders what would have happened if we had kept the baby. She is convinced that was the girl we had prayed for.

Planned Visit from Michigan Family

Even though my parents had flown out from Michigan in June shortly after the stroke, they wanted to keep their plans for a return trip in August, so my parents, grandma, and sister came to visit along with my nephew Landon, who was only one at the time. Even though Michele was aware her baby was no more, she remembers being confused. During my family's visit, Landon had been placed on her lap, and she wondered, "Is this my baby? Is this the baby that was in my tummy? But he's too big to be mine. My baby is gone." It's amazing that despite the severity of her brain injury, she was still able to think logically, no matter how heartbreaking the subject.

CHAPTER 4

The Hills and the Valleys

As admission time to the SNF came, excitement was buzzing. It meant that she was one step closer to the final discharge. We were also glad she was sent to that particular location because it was a lot closer to our home. It was only a 15-minute drive and didn't require getting on the freeway. At the same time, it was hard to have her there because Michele was the youngest resident by far; all the others were at least forty years older. We kept hearing, "At least Michele is young," and that a young brain has more plasticity. The older people get, the harder it is for them to recover from a stroke. That really didn't make it easier to cope with, though. Nobody knew what Michele's outcome would be, and it felt like people were giving us a false sense of hope.

As Michele healed, our relationship grew deeper and our worship in the Lord became richer. Some visits had us singing at the top of our lungs with music turned up on my phone, hands raised in the air. In fact, that was when Michele first spoke after the stroke. Her first words were in a song, singing praises to the Giver of Life, the One who gave Michele a second chance.

Our generally positive reaction to the stroke was not due to our own strength. Early on, God gave me a vision that our story could be used for something powerful. I knew He had a plan. It was the Holy Spirit that held us together. Paul writes in 2 Corinthians 12:9-10, "And He has said to me, 'My grace is sufficient for you, for power is perfected in weakness.' Most gladly, therefore, I will rather boast about my weaknesses, so that the power of Christ may dwell in me. Therefore, I am well content with weaknesses, with insults, with distresses, with persecutions, with difficulties, for Christ's sake; for when I am weak, then I am strong."

Hard Times Ahead

Michele was at the SNF when the reality of her disability finally sunk in. At first, she didn't understand why she couldn't just go home, but then at the facility she was transferred into a wheelchair for the first time. It was then that she realized she couldn't walk. Michele's physical therapist, Andrea, was like a breath of fresh air, though. Our first meeting with her had a positive impact on the whole family. She reframed Michele's mindset right away by telling her not to think of herself as being sick. Andrea wanted Michele out of the hospital gown she'd worn for the last three and a half months and into regular clothes. We could tell that Andrea truly cared about her and wanted to do everything she could to help her improve. She made it a personal goal to take Michele on as her patient. As the manager of the therapy, Andrea didn't have many people she personally helped, but Michele held a sweet spot in her heart. Maybe it was because they were both moms with kids of similar ages. Whatever the reason, we were thankful for what she did. However, we weren't quite as pleased with some other things there.

Michele was transferred to the SNF on a Friday, and we quickly learned how the nursing care was run. The support was lacking tremendously compared to the hospital, and the weekends were especially difficult as they operated with only a skeleton crew. We were told that's just the way it is in places like that. It was a wake-up call for all of us. The family agreed that having someone with Michele every day was non-negotiable for her safety; sometimes she would be waiting for over an hour after she pushed her call light before a nurse would attend to her. Because we grew tired of the constant waiting, we quickly learned how to care for her ourselves in whatever ways we could. I felt bad for the other residents who didn't have the level of support Michele did. I would constantly hear them say that they'd been waiting for hours when they desperately needed help. Meanwhile, the workers appeared to just be in the hallways chit-chatting. I knew that if the other residents were treated that way, Michele was probably treated similarly when we weren't there.

While Michele was a resident at the SNF, 911 was called on two separate occasions, and both of those times were because we thought Michele had another stroke. During the first of those instances, I witnessed Michele steadily lose consciousness, which obviously frightened me. She was taken to the ER, and the staff performed a head CT and an EEG—a test that detects abnormalities in your brain waves—which both came back relatively normal. With the encouraging tests and vitals, the doctor felt Michele would be okay; we waited for her to come around, and then she was discharged from the ER and sent up to the ward.

I was never given answers about what caused the sudden relapse; I don't think the doctors really knew. However, I had my suspicions that Michele was accidentally overdosed. I had paid a visit to the SNF earlier on, and I noticed significant errors in the way they tracked her medication as I looked over her chart. I went to the manager with this observation and insisted that they make her medication schedule available to me at all times. Unfortunately, they still weren't good about updating it. I'm sure management was tired of meeting with us so often, but I didn't care. Michele deserved better treatment than what she was getting. The other residents deserved better treatment too.

Overcoming Setbacks

Michele remained at the hospital for a week or so before she was sent back to the SNF. Although we had kept a watchful eye on Michele's care prior to the incident, our guard went up even more after that. With all the inconsistencies, we scheduled yet another meeting with the manager. We expressed our concern, and she apologized and informed us things would change. Of course, we were beyond skeptical at this point. We asked if there were any other places Michele could go, but the alternatives presented to us didn't sound much better. We ultimately decided to remain there. Although much of the care was lacking, the therapy was good. Michele was being challenged and had been making progress.

Despite the setbacks caused by the ER visit, the grind of PT continued, and it was awesome to see the advancements Michele made over time. She graduated from being transferred by a Hoyer lift to a slide transfer with a transfer board. As she progressed, we were updated on how to maneuver her. She also gained enough strength in her core to sit at the edge of the bed. Andrea made the experience fun for the family. As part of her therapy, Michele would sit upright by herself and play games with the kids. Some pretty intense games of Connect Four ensued! Michele was always competitive, and these times were no different. She ruthlessly battled the kids for the title of victor.

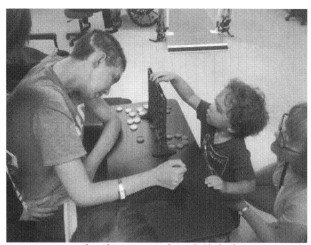

One core-strengthening exercise Michele was asked to do involved taking a playing card in her hand, finding its match on a board, and then reaching to pin the two cards together. This exercise was difficult but helpful for many reasons. Because Michele is now unable to see out of the left side of both her eyes, she needed to get in the habit of scanning her eyes from side to side. This is important for navigating the wheelchair through doorways or seeing if anything dangerous is coming at her head from her blind spots. The exercise was also good for increasing her balance. Michele thought it was a waste of time, saying, "Why are you having me do this? Why don't you just let me try to walk?" She may not have been fully aware of the seriousness of her injuries at that point. After all, her brain was still healing.

Bringing in the Boys

It was always an adventure when all three boys came. Luckily, Michele was still in a room by herself that overlooked the courtyard where the boys would go run around. We were so glad they had it to relieve some energy. The courtyard was a beautiful area, a great place for the residents to go where they could experience some normalcy. There were also common areas with tables, games, and a TV. We would get Michele into her wheelchair and spend lots of time in those common areas.

We tried to maintain our Saturday pizza movie nights, which had been a family tradition for years prior to the stroke. I would set up the laptop on a table and the boys would take turns snuggling with their mom in her bed while the rest of us sat in chairs besides her. Really, the only difference was that we didn't have pizza.

The boys liked coming for another reason as well: ice cream! The staff loved to spoil them with sweets. Once Michele was cleared to eat, it was similar for her; her favorite was any flavor sorbet they had. I think she completely wiped out their supply.

Andrea was always excited to show the boys some new things Michele was able to do in therapy. Having the boys there served two purposes; they motivated mom to work hard, and the boys could see how hard mom was working. Andrea had a special therapy time scheduled that we could watch, and we all made a great effort to be there. I took time off work and was accompanied by the boys and her parents. We couldn't wait to see her in action! However, things didn't always progress the way we thought they would.

Déjà Vu

The second time an ambulance was called to pick up Michele from the SNF, it was again because her mental condition had quickly declined. This time, we all witnessed her go downhill until she became unresponsive. As we watched them push Michele on the gurney, I saw Conner cry for the first time since the stroke. This nine-year-old kid had remained strong through it all, but seeing his mom on the gurney again had to have been like déjà vu. I'm sure the memory of her leaving in the first ambulance was still fresh in his mind.

As they loaded her into the vehicle, I hugged the boys and told them mom was going to be okay. I'm glad Michele's parents were with them, so I could ride in the ambulance with her. Because this was a repeat occurrence, I wanted to make sure I was there to talk with the doctors. Upon arrival, the same protocol as before was followed; head CT and EEG. Both of those tests again came back normal, and my suspicions of overdose grew.

When things settled down a bit at the hospital, I called Michele's mom to see how the kids were doing. Conner was not okay. It wasn't like him to show his emotions in that way, but he was crying pretty hard on the phone. I talked with him for a few minutes, and I felt his anxiety. He remained upset until I called back later with good news; Michele's loss of consciousness was not caused by another stroke, which is what we were worried about. We praised the Lord, and Conner was immediately relieved.

While I was waiting with Michele in her room, I sent a group text to my inner circle of men. One of them was with the local Sheriff's Department, who just happened to be nearby. He rushed over and found us in a room in the back of the ER. I was not doing well; we had already been through so much. I told him I was worried. A short while after he left, Michele started to come to. As before, she was monitored for a few hours and then sent up to the ward. After a few days, she was discharged from the hospital and sent back to the SNF.

It was difficult knowing that she would probably have setbacks again. She had worked so hard, only to regress. Isn't that like life? You make progress but get knocked down, and by the time you get back up, you notice that you're further back than when you started. That's where perseverance comes in, right? A lot of people would throw in the towel at this point, but not Michele. Not my family. We kept going. But let me make this clear; we were only able to because He gave us strength to rise and take the next steps in faith. He remained the light in our dark tunnel.

Weeks after Michele returned to the SNF, she told me she heard everything that was said in the ER when my friend visited the hospital. She remembers being really scared, hearing us crying, and me telling my friend that I was worried. Michele wanted to respond, but she couldn't. She thought she was going to die.

Lions and Tigers and Firefighters, Oh My!

Once again, it was time for Michele to return to the SNF, and my boxing gloves were on. We practically camped there the rest of her stay. Besides the stroke scares, there were other interesting things that happened at that facility as well. Her parents were out of the country on a business trip, and I was with the kids when I received a phone call from Michele late one night, saying she smelled smoke and was worried a fire had started in the building. I promptly called a friend to watch the kids, so I could go be with her. When I arrived at the SNF, I noticed the facility was without power. I also smelled electrical smoke. I went to Michele's room and found her in a very uncomfortable position. Michele had an air mattress that required power to be inflated, and unsurprisingly, the facility did not have a backup generator. At least her CNAs had put pillows underneath her, so she wasn't just lying on a metal frame. Michele filled me in on what was going on. Before I had arrived, the thick electrical smoke caused her tremendous anxiety, since she couldn't get out of bed and head for safety. She could see firefighters and the other residents walking back and forth in the hallway in front of her room and was scared she would be left behind.

After confirming there wasn't danger to the building, the firefighters left. Apparently, the smoke was caused by a rat that had gotten into the transformer box and chewed through the wires. Talk about a crispy critter. The smoke soon cleared, but it took a while for the power to return; meanwhile, only the layer of pillows propped Michele up. I stayed with her for as long as I could, but eventually left to relieve our friend from watching the kids.

Field Trip

One benefit of Michele being a resident at the SNF was that we could take her out for the day. When her therapists felt like she was strong enough, we made plans to bring her out to the world.

Since she was unable to stand on her own, we needed to help her in and out of the car, so one of the PTs gave us a crash course on how to do a stand pivot transfer. It was very intimidating at first. I worried about twisting her knee or ankle. Dropping her was also a concern. Since she couldn't lift her foot because of the paralysis, we had to twist her foot while we twisted her body. Fortunately, we're pros at this point since we've been doing it for over five years.

Having Michele in the car again was an amazing feeling; it was like she was graduating. It was hard for Michele though because the vision loss made her very nauseous. We also needed to stuff pillows around her because she didn't have the strength to fully support her core while being tossed around during the drive.

The first stop we made as a family of five once again was to

Conner's soccer game. As we pulled up to our church's field, everything felt surreal. I was glad to have her parents there to help. Dan was there waiting for us, and he unloaded the wheelchair as I prepared Michele for the transfer. Moving her to the wheelchair from the car was easier than the other way around; gravity worked with us since the wheelchair was lower.

It was incredible to push Michele out on that field. We saw our friends, and they were overjoyed to see us together outside a hospital setting. Conner was also very excited that his mom was there to watch him play. I'm sure he wanted to show off for her. He dribbled down the field and took a shot at the goal, almost scoring his first goal of the season. Michele had a difficult time following the back and forth action, but she was excited to be there to support Conner nonetheless. Once the game was over, we knew we had to take Michele back to the SNF. I can't say the thought about kidnapping her never crept in.

We were able to take Michele out on one other trip while she was a resident, and that time we went to church. I can't even tell you the emotions we both felt as we headed down the aisle for the first time since everything happened. We were publicly acknowledged by the pastor, and it was great to see all the people who had showered us with love and support.

After church, we took Michele to one more place: home. A friend from church built a custom ramp, so we could push Michele into the house, and finally doing so was overwhelming. I can't even imagine what Michele felt. Her favorite chair in the living room had been vacant until that day. I transferred her into it and the boys gathered around her. Mom was home!! It just wasn't the same with her gone. We knew it was temporary, but that didn't stop us from totally enjoying the time she was there. We had to take Michele back to the SNF much too quickly, but we were excited to think about when she would return home for good. We knew what steps she needed to take to prepare both herself and us for that, so she worked hard every day towards that goal.

The Accident of the Century

I frequently got phone calls from Michele at the SNF. They were mostly at night, telling me that she was waiting for extended periods of time to get help again. We gave Michele the number to the front desk, so she had another way to get a hold of the staff. The call button didn't seem to be enough.

One night, Michele called the front desk and her nurse picked up. Michele wanted to know how much longer it would be until someone was able to come to her. The nurse was evidently annoyed by the phone call and spoke in an incredibly rude way. Michele called me after, telling me what had happened. Well alright then. I rolled up my sleeves and called the front desk myself. The same nurse picked up. "I told you somebody was coming," she snapped, thinking it was Michele. "You need to wait!" She didn't even say hello or ask who it was. I waited to speak, appalled with her attitude. Sorry, lady, you just spoke with the wrong dude. She got a piece of my mind that night. I followed up with the manager the next morning as well. I'm not sure what happened to her after that, but I do know she was promptly called into a meeting.

Back to School

It was soon time for the kids to return to school. Conner was in fourth grade and Easton was entering Kindergarten. I know how important it was to Michele to be there when school started. She was crushed that she couldn't participate, but we planned for the boys to go visit her afterward, so they could tell her about their day.

It was hard that Michele couldn't go on the first day for all of us. The boys wanted her there; they were starting at a new place. Fortunately, that place was our church, and we knew they would be around people that loved them and knew our situation. The teachers were wonderful and kept tabs on the boys, reporting back to us if they felt like the kids were struggling.

Her Swallow Returns

Remember reading how we were told Michele would never be able to swallow again? One thing the doctors may not have realized is that we knew the Great Physician, and He is not to be put in a box. There is no limit to what our God can do.

The speech therapist at the SNF was working closely with Michele. At first, she introduced ice chips. Michele recalls the pure bliss she felt when the ice chips touched her tongue. This was the first time anything had been in her mouth besides a tube or suction in several months. She was hooked; it was all she wanted after that. Her speech therapist was extra cautious with her, though. She wasn't allowed to have them except under close observation. The next thing introduced to her was soup. It was so exciting to see her making progress with something the doctors were convinced she would never do again.

Michele was given exercises to strengthen her throat muscles. She was working towards her swallow study, the Modified Barium Swallow. That was the test she needed to "pass" in order to be cleared to eat. Michele was told to have a reward in mind for when she had a successful swallow study. She chose a frosty from Wendy's. I believe that gave her motivation to push through the difficulties. She came closer and closer to reaching that goal after a couple of months of persistence. As each week went by, the speech therapist noticed positive changes with her swallow. They gradually introduced different textures, testing her strength. Finally, they agreed it was time to schedule the study she had been waiting for.

The day of the Modified Barium Swallow came at last. On the way to the hospital for the appointment, we were both excited for Michele to blow the study out of the water. I asked the staff if I could be in the room with Michele, so I could see the results. The speech pathologist mixed the barium with a cracker for the first attempt. I watched the screen, barely able to control my excitement. Michele chewed the cracker and pushed it down her throat. It went correctly! Success! I knew it right away. I jumped up and down, trying to contain my loud voice as I punched my fist into the air. Michele saw me and started beaming. She knew the results were good. I tried to maintain composure after that, since Michele wasn't done yet, and she needed to focus. The pathologist graduated her to liquid. We waited. Yes!! There was no aspiration! Praise God!

After the study, the pathologist confirmed that Michele's swallow was back. He cautioned her, though. He said her swallow was delayed and that she needed to be careful, but that she was moving in the right

direction. Michele was given clearance to eat a restricted diet. Orders were written for her diet and sent to the SNF. Next stop, Wendy's! As we celebrated Michele's progression, we found joy in the small things. It's so easy to take them for granted. Each win was huge for her, no matter how insignificant they may have seemed to someone else.

Michele's stomach tube was left in, since that was how she was given all her meds. They dissolved the pills and pushed them through with a syringe. Her nourishment was maintained through the G-tube as well, but she was now cleared to have trays of food sent to her room. She was super excited to order "real" food. Because of the restrictions, her food still needed to be puréed, but I don't think she cared that much—until they brought in a puréed cheeseburger. Let's just say it looked very "interesting."

The Last Stop Before Home

The ticket to getting out of the SNF was almost in hand; the next phase of Michele's recovery was going to the Rehabilitation Institute of Oregon (RIO). We knew it would be a process for her to get accepted, though. Because RIO is an intensive inpatient program, a representative needed to come out beforehand and interview Michele to ensure she could handle their demanding schedule. She needed to be able to support herself in the standing frame for a specified amount of time and have enough endurance to withstand an entire day of therapy. With those requirements in mind, Michele's team of therapists were determined to get her to that level of ability as soon as possible.

Finally, an appointment with a representative from RIO was scheduled, and we all presented our best selves to her. RIO wanted to make sure that Michele had plenty of family support before giving her access to their world-class facility. The representative observed

Michele during a therapy session, talked with us, and headed back to her office. The prayers continued, and they worked! Michele was officially approved to be a patient at RIO, and we were elated. Now she only had to wait for a room to open. Each step of the way felt like another graduation.

It was the beginning of October when the time came for the biggest transfer since the stroke to occur. On average, patients are only granted two weeks of admission to RIO before discharge, but the Lord showed favor to Michele. She was approved to stay there for four weeks. We waited for the ambulance to arrive at the SNF since it was required for transfer between facilities. I was on a first-name basis with one of the drivers by that point.

Michele arrived at RIO on the weekend and, once again, was given her own room. This room was massive compared to what we were used to. She had large windows with a nice view of Portland. The room itself was such a blessing, especially when the kids came. There was more room for them to spread out with whatever activity we brought for them while visiting.

All the nurses at RIO were amazing. A speech therapist was among the first to see Michele. She wanted to know how strong Michele's swallow was, so she administered some tests with different food consistencies. The therapist believed that Michele should graduate to solid food. No more purée! We were both super excited. The first meal she had was macaroni and cheese. I'll bet that was the best plate of mac and cheese she ever had.

The first weekend was spent getting acclimated to her new surroundings and preparing for Monday. We were excited about the possibilities before us. On a tour of the facility, we saw one room that had a track on the ceiling, which we discovered is used to help patients learn how to walk again. Patients get into a harness, a bungee cord-like strap is attached to the track, and then they are supported from above. It utilizes a zero-gravity system to take away the fear and risk of the patient falling, allowing them to push themselves as they put one foot in front of the other. We knew this was coming up for Michele and were excited to put it to use.

In addition to the weight machines, RIO had another piece of equipment that piqued our interest. It was a bike with lots of wires. We learned the bike was used to measure how much force each leg was exerting; the physical therapist would hook up the wires to a patient in a wheelchair while they pedaled. There was also a screen on the bike that gave the patient something to focus on. It would often show a moving road as they pedaled to give the impression that they were going somewhere.

During occupational therapy, a full kitchen was used for the patients to relearn skills they lost during their injury. It was the therapists' goal to get Michele as functional as possible, and the kitchen was high on the list of to-dos. They also had a bedroom, which was used to practice transferring. Because we needed to transfer Michele into and out of the bed, we planned to use this room quite a bit. Since we had been so involved with her care by that time, we knew how she liked to be positioned in bed. She wasn't able to roll over on her own, so we would roll her onto each side during the night. We wanted to work on that at RIO also though because we didn't have a hospital bed with guard rails at home. RIO wants the family to be well-equipped to take the patient home just as much as they want the patient to be ready to go home.

Weekly meetings were set up with the key staff members, so each person could state where Michele had made progress and where she still needed to improve. I attended as many of those as I could with her. It was encouraging to hear their reports. It was at RIO that Michele had the most gains, and fast. A couple of weeks went by before she was put in the zero-gravity harness, but once she was, she took off. They set up the system so that she was supporting sixty percent of her body weight, but if Michele ever got tired, the harness would catch her. The therapist saw that Michele was doing most of the work, though, so she was given more of the load. Towards the end of our stay at RIO, Michele was walking along the handrails of the hospital without a harness. Her left leg needed help to advance because of the paralysis from the stroke, but she was able to bear her own weight!

Michele also got a chance to use the bike with all the wires, and we learned that Michele was able to push each leg with the same amount of force. That was really exciting for us. It meant that some muscles in her left leg were still able to fire.

Throughout the stay at RIO, the feeding tube was kept in place to make sure Michele stayed hydrated, but she continued eating solid foods. She had her favorites. Once she discovered they had sorbet, they couldn't keep it stocked. Michele ate their supply! Along with sorbet, chicken tenders were a favorite. Before the tube was pulled, Michele had to demonstrate that she could drink enough fluids, and finally, on November 2, 2017, she was cleared by the doctors to have the tube removed. The sucker was yanked out of her belly that very day. When the nurse had tried to prepare us for what was to come, she just told us that she was going to pull it out. Michele and I were like, "Wait, what? Just pull it out?" "Yup," the nurse replied. She prepped the area, made sure she had enough gauze, gripped the tube, and pulled. Crazy! We heard a popping sound as it was removed. In a way, getting the feeding tube out was like Michele being removed from another umbilical cord. It provided her nourishment from an outside source, like a mother supporting a baby inside the womb. This was another milestone in her recovery; another glimpse of light. She had come so far.

November 2nd was also the day Michele was discharged. She was homeward bound, for good! On one hand, we were overwhelmingly excited to get her back home, but on the other, we knew she had momentum that we wanted to keep going. For all the people that went through RIO, the caveat was that they had to be making progress. That was another purpose for the weekly meetings. But Michele was! I highly doubt that she was at the peak; we both wonder if she would've gotten more strength back had she stayed a little longer.

CHAPTER 5

Home at Last

When the time came for Michele to be sent home, I was gripped with anxiety. She was given pages and pages of prescription medicine along with her discharge papers. It was now up to us to take care of her. Until that point, we had help (for the most part). As I read the discharge instructions, I saw the schedule for her medications. That only added to the amount of overwhelm; I knew that if I messed up in that area, Michele would be in a world of pain. Easton had a great idea to prepare for Michele's homecoming. He wanted to decorate the house to make it extra special. Some friends of ours took him shopping and bought decorations they knew she would love. He wanted to make sure the homecoming was amazing.

Home

When the wheelchair-accessible van arrived to take Michele away from the hospital, it became more apparent that we would have to adapt to a new way of living. To this day, Michele isn't able to stand up and get in a car; we transfer her.

I missed the initial reactions from the family as Michele entered the house to stay. I still needed to get her prescriptions filled, so I turned around and drove to the clinic. I must have been there for hours waiting for them to be filled. There were so many. I had a really hard time with it. Before the stroke, Michele was careful about not taking any medicine unless absolutely necessary. She would even avoid taking Tylenol if she could. The scripts she was given were necessary, though. The stroke really did a number on her whole body.

When my turn had come to check out, I was inundated with anxiety and worry. As the pharmacist pulled each drug out of the bag and set it on the counter, I broke down in tears. I had no idea how I was going to handle this. I didn't want Michele to suffer because of me; I wanted to do her medications right. I saw how her body responded when she didn't get what she needed; because of the extensive nerve damage, Michele could have intense leg spasms. These spasms twist, jerk, and contract her entire leg. Sometimes they get so bad you can hear popping, which sounds like her bones are cracking. These spasms can be extremely painful for her, and they are usually controlled by medicine. I had also seen how her body responded when she was given too much, thanks to the SNF. I didn't want her to suffer any more from my incompetence. I felt the task was too much for me to handle.

I could tell the pharmacist felt sorry for me. She was compassionate and sympathetic. It appeared difficult for her to continue as well. Each prescription taken out of the bag made the weight on my shoulders feel heavier and heavier. She asked if I had any questions. Feeling completely overwhelmed, no questions came to mind.

At home the next day, I called Rich, one of our friends who was a doctor, and told him how stressed I was. He offered to come over and make a house call. During his visit, we looked at all her meds and decided which ones we could combine. It just didn't seem sustainable to give her medicine six different times each day. By the time he left, our medicine schedule was reduced to four times a day. It may not have been a big shift, but it was enough to make it manageable.

The boys loved having their momma home. They would take turns laying with her at night and snuggling. Michele loved being home as well, but things were different. The noise level from having three boys in the home can be enough to drive you bonkers. Just ask their grandparents! That was the case for Michele. She wasn't used to having all the commotion anymore. The sounds she had grown accustomed to during the previous six months had come from the devices she was hooked up to. Also, because of the brain damage and the removal of a section of her brain, most stimuli would cause her to have massive headaches. Some of the tasks she always did before, like reading books to the boys or playing games with them, are now extremely challenging for her. Thankfully, she can still read. If the books are easy enough, she will gladly do it for the boys. It's good to look for the silver lining with all situations, or that glimmer of light while you remain in the tunnel. For us, we were thankful she still had the ability to talk. If the bleeding had been on the left side of her brain, she may have lost the ability to speak or read, but because it occurred on the right, there were still things Michele could do to be a part of the boys' life.

Michele wanted to participate at the boys' school too, so we scheduled a day for her to be a teacher's assistant. The students and the teachers alike were encouraged by her presence there. Their prayers were answered. While Michele was in the hospital, Easton's teacher asked me to come in and explain to her class what had happened to Michele. She wanted the class to hear from me what they had been praying for. When Michele showed up at school to help, the students were able to see a tangible prayer request answered.

Home Health

Michele was set up for home health therapy right away. A physical therapist, occupational therapist, and speech therapist were all assigned to her. She was blessed to have such an outstanding team. Up until this point, her right foot had puzzled all her therapists.

They weren't sure how to correct her foot from being hyperextended and rotated inward, and that posed a problem for her recovery. She couldn't bear weight on her left leg because of the paralysis, and when she put weight on her right foot, there was an increased risk of rolling her ankle. Her occupational therapist took it as a challenge to fix her foot's position. She decided to do serial casting, which wasn't in her job description. That meant that Michele's foot would be fixed into the best position we could get and then cast. We had to loosen up the muscles in her leg. Michele would have the cast on for a week or two, then, after it was removed, the therapists stretched her foot and the process was repeated. After about three sets of casts, Michele's occupational therapist was able to get her foot flat on the floor. This allowed them to kick it up a gear with the therapy. After a few months of focused therapy, Michele could walk about a hundred feet. A hemi-walker was used to help her balance. On nice days, they even brought Michele outside to do her therapy. It was amazing to see how strong she had become since the stroke.

Just in Time for the Holidays

It was such a blessing to have Michele home in time for Thanksgiving and Christmas. Yet, at the same time, it was hard. With Christmas, came an overwhelming feeling of grief, as we mourned the baby we had lost after the stroke.

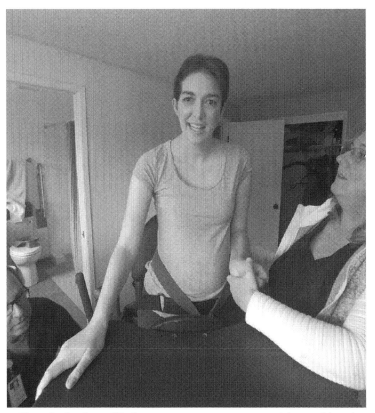

Shortly before Christmas, a poem was read by a friend at their son's memorial service. His car had veered off the road and collided head-on with a tree. The parents had to make the decision to pull life support from their son. The poem is called, "My First Christmas in Heaven" (the poem is included at the end of the book). We didn't know their son personally, but we were deeply impacted by the remembrance of his life.

I admired his mom's strength as she read the poem. They are an amazing family and strong believers in the Lord. It's incredible how so much hope can be found during a time of suffering. That family had every right to be angry and resentful at the Lord. They could've shaken their fists at Him and questioned their faith—but they held fast to their faith instead. That family is an awesome example of how to trust the Lord while you remain in the tunnel.

I read the poem before we ate a Christmas meal that the church prepared for us. It felt fitting to read it having lost our baby. That child experienced Christmas with Jesus for the first time that year. It took me a while to read through it fully, as I was overcome with emotion. The attempt to push through to the end caused my tears to flow even more.

It was a somber Christmas that year in several ways, but there was still a lot to be thankful for. It was so good to have the whole family finally together and at home for the holidays.

The Second Brain Surgery

We were so grateful our insurance company agreed for Michele's surgery to be performed outside their network. We were positive that Dr. Deshmukh was the right person for the job. It took some time before they agreed to pay for it, but they did, and that's what mattered.

There were two different variations of the bypass Dr. Deshmukh could perform: direct and indirect revascularization. The direct approach was more invasive than the other; it involved cutting the cerebral artery that was responsible for the malformation and clamping off both sides. They would then take a segment from an artery in her leg and graft it in. This process is like a cardiac bypass graft. The other, more indirect version of the surgery is called an on-lay. This is where they would take some healthy tissue from her scalp and lay it on the troubled area. It would take up to six months for this method to be fully effective, but both approaches would ultimately have the same result.

One of the elders at church reserved an entire row for our family every Sunday. He put signs on the bench that read, "Reserved for the Rezewski Family." The Sunday before the surgery, a good friend, Marci, placed some encouraging notes along the bench we sat on. They were heart-shaped and included passages meant to give us hope and remind us not to worry.

Up until the morning of the surgery, Dr. Deshmukh planned on performing the direct approach, but after much thought, he opted to go with the indirect method instead. Michele was asymptomatic on the left side of her brain, and Dr. Deshmukh was worried about the high risk. He felt confident the six months it would take for the indirect approach to take effect was the better way to go. As the nurse rolled Michele out of the exam room on the way to the OR, I called for Dr. Deshmukh. I wanted him to know that we were praying for him during the surgery. I didn't know if he was a believer; I didn't care. God still uses those who don't believe in Him. He thanked me and said, "I appreciate that." I then went to the waiting room with Michele's parents and a friend from the church that came to be with us.

The surgery was successful! It wasn't nearly as invasive as the first one Michele endured immediately after the stroke. Dr. Deshmukh did an amazing job. The incision was just at her hairline and ran down to her left ear. With her hair grown back, you can't even tell it's there.

After the surgery was completed, it was apparent Michele had taken a few steps back in her recovery, but that was expected. Fortunately, the steps back were minor in comparison to what they could have been. I noticed the tone was back in her left leg; it was as stiff as a board following the surgery. Thankfully, I knew how to fix that due to watching so much therapy. I worked her leg through the full range of motion. There was a lot of resistance at first, but once I broke that up, it was basically back to how it was before the surgery.

It took a couple of weeks for her to regain the strength and the mobility she lost at that point, during which time she stayed at the hospital. When discharge came, we had to decide whether to have her go back to the SNF or bring her home. This decision was a no-brainer for us: HOME! Especially with what had happened previously, we felt confident we could take care of her at home. Within a couple of days, home health therapy resumed, and her mobility was back to the way it was before the surgery not long after.

About six months post-op, Michele was scheduled for a cerebral angiogram to see how well her brain had responded to the surgery. After it was completed, Dr. Deshmukh called us back to explain the results. He was well-pleased. Her brain was receiving adequate blood flow; the on-lay procedure had worked! However, Michele still needs to go in for annual studies to make sure a defect hasn't returned. Moyamoya disease is non-curable, but it is treatable. We just need to be careful.

CHAPTER 6

Some Backstory

Even prior to Michele's stroke, we were not strangers to suffering. On September 5, 2009, we lost our first child. We were married for about four and a half years; Conner was one and a half. Michele was twenty weeks pregnant when she felt like something was wrong with the baby. After a few days of not feeling him kick, she grew concerned and couldn't shake the bad feeling she had. We scheduled an appointment with her OB/GYN, and he confirmed Michele's suspicion. The baby's heart had stopped. The doctor sent Michele for a second opinion, just to make sure, before a D&C was performed. The second test confirmed the first. Our grief didn't stop there; we were told the only way for the baby to come out was for Michele to deliver him naturally.

After a confirmation ultrasound, Michele was sent to the hospital, and placed in the delivery room. She endured the typical birthing process; epidural, breathing, pushing, waiting, and more breathing and pushing. The baby was delivered as a stillborn.

We gave him a name: Jacob. He was small enough to fit in the palm of your hand. One leg was longer than the other, and there was a thick band around one of his arms. As friends came in to see us and offer their support, Michele and I took turns holding him. Saying "goodbye" to Jacob was hard, but we knew we'd see him again in heaven without any deformities.

In the pregnancy's early stages, Michele had been watched closely. Her doctor had thought there were twins at first because he saw two gestational sacs, which was later called a hematoma. We learned that there was a risk to the baby because of the hematoma, but there wasn't anything we could do about it except pray. Sometimes when we pray, God's answer is "no." That just means He has bigger plans for those unanswered prayers. We know that God had a bigger purpose for Jacob than to let him be here with us. Pain and suffering are not for naught—they have a purpose, even if we don't know what that purpose is during times of trial.

On September 22, 2009, shortly after we had lost Jacob, my eight-year enlistment in the US Air Force came to an end. The military was a hard lifestyle for us, and my term ended terribly. My commanding officer would not approve me for reenlistment. I had made some mistakes with paperwork that cost the Air Force money. The truth is, the training I received when I switched career fields was very inadequate. I was not set up for success. Because of those mistakes, my dreams of spending twenty years in the Air Force ended.

Looking back, I now know that losing that dream was a blessing in disguise. If I had still been enlisted when Michele had the stroke, I would have had to separate under a hardship discharge. Also, there was the possibility I may have been deployed then. I cannot imagine being away from home and learning about the stroke from a phone call.

Up until my enlistment ended, we were living on base in privatized housing. We had to pack up our house, clean it like crazy to pass the stringent home inspection, find a new place to live, and get a new job. All the while, we were mourning Jacob's death. Michele's parents were gracious enough to let us move into their home. We were there for one year. Michele, Conner, me, and oh, let's not forget Bailey. He was our dog; a German Shepherd, Border Collie, Rottweiler, Shar Pei mix. All four of us slept in a room in the basement. Thankfully it was a large room, so we weren't very crammed.

I never really had time to grieve the loss of Jacob. I had to move on quickly with the new job. We all struggled during this time, and even though we didn't know what was to come, I believed losing Jacob helped prepare us for what was ahead with Michele's stroke. During this time, I drew closer to God than I had ever before. My hunger for His word grew stronger. It's amazing how God uses the hard things in our life to strengthen our relationship with Him. It's so easy to get caught up in thinking this life is too hard. Just remember, it's the hard times during which you are being strengthened.

The Move that Would Save Michele's Life

Fast-forward to 2013. My graduation from X-ray school was approaching, and the job market wasn't looking very good. There were at least four different schools in the area pumping out X-ray techs, and it looked like everything was saturated. I applied for jobs all over. We were in Spokane, Washington, which is the first place I looked for jobs. I also looked in Colorado, Montana, Oregon, all over Washington, and other places. On July 16, our anniversary, I had an interview with the Portland VA Medical Center. I found out a couple of weeks later that I got the job. I started in October that year.

We packed up from Spokane and headed to Oregon. As we pulled out of the driveway, Michele's dad said he knew there was a reason we were moving there and that God had a plan. Boy, was he right. Had Michele's stroke occurred while we lived in Spokane, I don't believe the local hospitals would have been able to handle an injury so severe. She probably would've been airlifted to the closest trauma center, Seattle's Harborview. That delay might have killed her. As I mentioned before, we were told that if Michele had arrived at the hospital 10 to 15 minutes later, she would have died. It would have taken her longer to fly to Seattle from Spokane than that. Isn't God's plan amazing? Also, it's in Portland where we met Dr. Deshmukh, our Moyamoya expert. It wasn't by chance Michele was redirected to his hospital the day of her stroke. I truly believe that if Michele had been brought to the hospital they had first planned on, she would have died from that as well.

The Perfect House for Us

Our first home when we relocated to Oregon was an apartment in

Beaverton. While we were there, Michele was diligent about looking for homes for sale in the area. I had a one-year probation period with the VA until I became fully vetted. One of the houses Michele found online was a ranch style home in a small community. At the time, there was already a buyer, but somehow she stumbled across that same house later and it was available. The buyer had backed out of the deal! We went to go look at it and loved it.

That was the second house we looked at in the area. The first one was Michele's dream house. It was a beautiful 1900 farmhouse. There was only one thing that stopped us from buying it; there were two floors and the main bathroom was upstairs with the master bedroom. The other rooms were downstairs, and all the guests would have to go upstairs to use the bathroom. We didn't like how that was set up. Michele just had a bad feeling about it, even though she loved the house.

The house we bought, which was the second house we looked at, turned out to work well for Michele after the stroke. The rooms were wide open, all on one floor, and there was only one step to get into the house. All the adjustments we needed to make were relatively easy. We tore down the existing bathroom, expanded it, and built a roll-in shower. I also ripped up the carpet and replaced it with laminate flooring to make it easier to navigate the wheelchair. We were meant to buy that house.

CHAPTER 7

Miracles

I don't use the word "miracle" lightly. People tend to throw the word around way too much, and that's not my intention here. However, with some of the things that happened after Michele's stroke, there isn't any other word I can think of to describe them. In this chapter, I'm going to mention some of the miracles that have led us to where we are now. This chapter will give you a "behind the scenes" glimpse as to how things had happened. I may have mentioned some of the miracles earlier, but for perspective's sake, I wanted them to all be mentioned together.

The first miracle I'll address is how Conner came to call 911. Michele had just taken pizza out of the freezer for pizza movie night when she felt her brain "explode." She made it down the hall into the bedroom and laid down on the bed before falling unconscious. She recalls thinking, "I'm gonna die with the boys alone in the next room. They're going to be alone, and I'll be in here dead." So, she prayed to God to let her live—to give her a second chance. At that time, Easton came into the room to show her his new Lego creation, which woke her up enough to interact with him. She remembers saying, "Mom is really sick. I need you to leave me alone." But then, she thought, "Crap, I'm going to go unconscious again," and told Easton to get Conner. By the time Conner came into the room, Michele was hanging slightly off the bed, in a postured position. (Posturing describes a person who has had severe brain damage. Their body becomes stiff, arms are bent, and fists are clenched.) Before Michele faded to black again, she told Conner that she was going to go unconscious. She also said, "My phone isn't calling 911, so I need you to call 911." She had tried to dial herself, but her phone happened to be doing a system update that rendered it completely useless.

More ideas came to Michele's mind before she was completely out. She thought about sending Conner to the neighbor's house for help but didn't want to do that because they had just moved in, and we didn't know them very well. She wasn't sure if they were good people. Michele also thought about sending Conner across the street to a different neighbor's house, but before she could do that, she fell unconscious.

It's amazing Conner had the composure to do as he was told while remaining calm. Michele's phone finished its update, and he called 911 as instructed. While he was on the phone with a dispatcher, Michele had the seizure. He told the dispatcher that she was "shaking and vibrating" on the bed. He kept his composure as he witnessed *all* of that. When the dispatcher asked for our address, Conner couldn't remember right away, but he was thinking clearly enough to look on the side of our house for the house number. The first responders were able to get there much sooner because of that, which was crucial; on top of the hemorrhagic stroke and seizure, Michele also had an ischemic stroke, so time was certainly of the essence. Amidst all this, Conner even thought to lock up our cat, so he didn't get away. How many adults would have responded that well, let alone a nine-year-old kid?

Because of his bravery and the way he jumped into action, Conner was nominated for the Red Cross Hero Award. He didn't end up receiving it, but he was actually happy about that. He didn't want the recognition. Conner told me, "What else was I supposed to do, dad?"

Another miracle was how Michele's friend, Shannon, was placed exactly where she needed to be, when she needed to be there. As she was driving, she was in the perfect location to see the fire truck turn down a street leading to our house. I believe the Holy Spirit gave her the instinct to follow. On top of all that, praise the Lord that Michele was at home when the stroke happened. What if she had been driving with all the kids in the car? That could have been tragic! But God allowed her to be home, with the kids safe, before her brain "exploded."

About a week or so after Michele's stroke, I went across the street to tell the neighbors what had happened. I assumed they had seen all the emergency vehicles in front of the house that day, and I wanted to fill in the gaps for them. They told me that two-year-old Kaiden had been pounding on the window so hard that our neighbor was going to come across the street and see what was going on. He was worried about Kaiden breaking the glass. However, before he could do so, the fire truck arrived along with the ambulance and sheriff.

I still wonder what it was like in the house with the first responders working on my wife in the back bedroom. We were told the deputies were good with the kids. They goofed around with the boys to distract them from what was going on. One of them even found a large ball with a handle, kind of like a seated Pogo stick, and started bouncing on it.

I'm not sure if this would be considered a miracle or not. Nonetheless, it happened by design. I was running late for work the day of Michele's stroke. That morning, she had told me, "I have never felt this anxious before." She wanted me to stay home; she had a feeling something was going to happen. But, because I didn't want to be late to work, I prayed with her, kissed her on the forehead, and walked out the door. I would have stayed had I known that was going to be the last time I saw her before she nearly died. I wonder how I would have responded had I been home and seen Michele the way Conner did. Would I have been calm, like Conner, and called 911 in time? Would we have been in the house? I might have taken the kids somewhere to give her a break by herself, which is something I often did when off work. I can't imagine coming back from playing at the park to find Michele dead.

The miracles continued after she was taken to the hospital too. I will never forget the words Dr. Antezana's assistant said: "If he didn't have *hope,* he wouldn't continue." I'm not sure any other staff members had the hope he had. As I was doing research for this book, I learned that they were making plans to harvest her organs in case she didn't make it. The day after, her surgeon noted that Michele had a "very poor prognosis." Michele was dealt cards that weren't in her favor, but that doesn't matter with God. He can take the most impossible situation and make it possible.

It was amazing how quickly Michele's parents arrived in Portland from Spokane. When they received the call from me, they just happened to be gathered for Bible study at *their* house. If they were at someone else's place, they may have been inclined to go home to grab a change of clothes before heading to the airport, and that delay may have prevented them from catching the flight. Also, there just *happened* to be someone there who could get them to the airport especially quickly. They just *happened* to board the last flight of the night and take the last two seats on the plane. Did those things really just happen by coincidence, though? I don't think so. Those things happened because it was according to His plan.

It was amazing to see prayers being answered in real time, even if they seemed small. For example, we planned a time for the boys to see mom about a week after the stroke occurred. Michele hadn't been able to open her eyes yet because the swelling was so profound. We prayed for her eyes to be opened—even just one eye. We wanted the boys to see mom look at them, and we wanted Michele to see her boys.

When it was time to bring the boys in, I was already with Michele. Their grandma and grandpa Conlon arrived with the boys, and I went out to meet them. Michele's eyes had remained shut to that point. Before I brought them back, I checked on her again and saw that she was starting to open her left eye! I excitedly ran down the hall and grabbed the boys. We brought the boys into the room, and her eye was open *all the way*! Michele's gaze tracked their movement, and the boys knew she'd seen them. It was little things like this that God used to show us His light as we traveled through our tunnel.

We were told that Michele had one of the worst brain bleeds the staff had ever seen, in which the patient survived. When she first responded to the verbal commands, the reaction from the nurses and doctors was priceless. There was also a lesion on her arm the doctors were worried about since it was suspected of having an MRSA infection, which, if left untreated, can become severe and cause sepsis. We prayed about that as well. Thankfully, the test came back negative, and the lesion went away on its own. Yet another answered prayer occurred when Michele was removed from life support after four days. She had been breathing on her own prior to that, but wasn't strong enough to be extubated. Then, after 11 days, she was removed from the oxygen—a total miracle.

Just for fun, I'll throw this little tidbit in there: the day Michele was removed from the ventilator, I asked her if she wanted a foot rub. She enthusiastically responded with a thumbs up! She had always loved getting foot rubs at home. It's hard not being able to give them to her now because of the extensive nerve damage; every time her feet are touched they spasm. But that time, there were no spasms.

CHAPTER 8

Ultimate Love

Up until this point, I have only briefly touched on all the help and support we received from our church body. In order to fully explain just how much they did for us, though, a devoted chapter is required. The support started the night of the stroke, but only grew from then on.

The Church Family God Ordained for Us

During the two weeks Michele stayed at the hospital in Portland, there was always someone there with us, whether we knew it or not. A good friend of mine from the men's Bible study and his wife, Tim and Tracey would come every day and sit in the waiting room, just in case we came out of Michele's room. They wanted to be there for us, but didn't want to take any time away from Michele. They sat there for hours, just waiting to see if we needed anything. That is love.

Many people came and treated me to lunch at the hospital cafeteria; the food was actually pretty good. We would sit, and they would let me talk and cry. There were a lot of tears shed, for sure.

They encouraged me along the way and wanted me to know that I wasn't alone. That is love.

Our church gave the two older boys a scholarship to Adventure Camp, which is sort of like Vacation Bible School, but with a Southwest Bible Church twist. Adventure Camp ran all day, Monday through Friday, for the entire summer. Each week had a different theme, and they went on field trips that matched each one. In the meantime, other friends were more than happy to help with our youngest, Kaiden, as he was too young to be at Adventure Camp. That is love.

Just like a "Turkish Market"

An amazing family in our church offered to have a yard sale at their house with the sole purpose of raising funds for anything that might come up during Michele's recovery. An article was put in the local news advertising the sale and asking for donations. They even came out to interview me about our story. I shared how "Conner is my rock through all of this." In addition to the yard sale, a GoFundMe campaign was created for our benefit.

The turnout was incredible. One of my friends from church described the scene as "a Turkish market." Another friend said, "(his) house looks like ants on a marshmallow. So many people, so much stuff. Praying for God to bring His hand to all those who serve and those who shop." People from all over the city were donating items. Some came just to give a cash donation without taking anything home. Here's a brief excerpt from Rich, the friend who owned the house where the yard sale was held:

> "This was an amazing day in many ways. All the support of those who donated truthfully very good items, people who came and read the Rezewski Family story and gave generously, poor families whom we are able to give clothing and other items to."

Then he continues to share about a conversation he had with someone checking out the sale. Here's what he said about that:

"The highlight of my day was a long conversation with a social worker who has not been to church in years.

"The social worker asked me, 'Why are you doing this?'

"I talked about our Friday morning group and about Brett and Michele's story. He told me he gets so discouraged with life, particularly all the foster care situations he encounters daily. I told him that many aspects of life beat us down on a daily basis, but we meet together to remind one another that life in Christ can and should be pursued in the midst of the demand of work and despite the brokenness of our world. The conversation was longer but at the end, he said this was the most encouraging conversation that he has had in years and asked about coming to the Friday morning group."

Then Rich said to me, "Brett, I do want you to know that what you are going through is being used by God, far beyond your capacity to comprehend. Your pain, Michele's bleed, is massive and terrible, but God is using your household for present and eternal purposes. The social worker is one example."

Because of the generosity and selfless acts of service, the funds from the yard sale and the GoFundMe campaign lasted three years; the money was used for physical therapy in a private gym. That is love.

Time to Roll Up Our Sleeves

A couple of guys in my men's Friday morning Bible study

group had the idea of organizing "work parties" at our home if anything needed to be done around the house. One of them came over one evening to do a walk-around and see how they could serve my family. He made a list and sent out a group message in the "Rezewski Family Support" chat (someone created this for me after the stroke) asking for volunteers. Truthfully, the response was overwhelming.

On June 24, 2017 (the same weekend the yard sale was going on), at least a dozen men and their kids showed up at my house on a mission. Admittedly, there were some things on their to-do list that I had neglected for years. By the end of the day, everything on that list had been crossed. That included six yards of bark chips spread around the front and back yards, assembling a grill I had purchased months prior to the stroke, laying sod on a portion of the front yard, cleaning the moss off the roof, hanging patio lights, pulling weeds in our flower bed, and cleaning the front pavers with a power washer. The kids banded together and helped pull weeds and spread out the bark chips. One friend, who is an absolute beast, fixed our fence that was about to topple over. They also fixed the gate and trimmed the shrubs. That is love.

Within days of the stroke, if not the day of, a "meal train" was started for our family. This meal train continued for two whole years. During each week, at least two generous meals were delivered to our house, often resulting in leftovers. Many times, some of Michele's home health therapy team were there when the meals were being delivered; they witnessed God's love as people came with bags of food. We shared the gospel with them many times. On occasion, our church body even brought extra snacks for the boys. For Thanksgiving in 2017 and 2018, our church collaborated and provided entire Thanksgiving meals, including a turkey. This was such a blessing, especially for Michele's mom. Connie has a servant's heart. She has tirelessly served our family with meals since they stopped being delivered. Dinner is always ready by the time I get home from work. That is love.

I want to highlight Rich and his family at least one more time. I am originally from Michigan, which is where my family currently lives. Rich and his wife had just completed remodeling their entire upstairs. They finished constructing the bedrooms and the bathroom about a week prior to Michele's stroke. He and his wife offered my family their home during their stay in Oregon.

My family usually travels in a pack that includes my parents, sister, and grandma. My sister, Lauren, *wasn't* a believer in Jesus at the time. I don't think she really knew what she was getting into by staying at their house. Rich and his wife are some of the most solid believers in Jesus I know. Their theology is sound; whenever they speak, people listen. The Lord has blessed them with wisdom most people don't have. They are the nicest people with so much love in their hearts that it overflows to everyone around them. They also made dinner for my family while they were there. I'm not sure exactly what the conversations included, but I have no doubt they centered on Jesus Christ and how, through our story, He revealed Himself in amazing ways. That is love.

While my family was visiting from Michigan, I wanted to take them to church and have them experience the outpouring of love our church family displayed. This was early on after the stroke, maybe a week later. That service was extremely emotional for me. The Worship Team played a song by Hillsong called "Broken Vessels." The waterworks started to flow just a few notes in. I'm pretty sure everyone in the sanctuary heard me. The family that had the idea for the yard sale sat behind us during the service, and they had compassion on me. They placed their hands on my shoulders and prayed for me.

Another work party was organized at my house a couple of weeks after the first; once again, the men assembled to bless our family. Some men who couldn't make it to the first one wanted in on the action. Or maybe it was just an excuse to get dirty. Maybe it was a little of both. At any rate, they blessed us. This time they worked inside and out: they unclogged my bathroom sink and shower drain; there was a hole that had been getting deeper over the years in the backyard, so they filled that in with soil and spread grass seed; we wanted a large bulletin hung up to help us stay organized with everything going on, so one friend took care of that; once again, more weeds were pulled.

A passage of scripture comes to mind as I recall all the things that were done to bless us. That is 1 Peter 4: 8-10, which reads, "Above all, keep fervent in your love for one another, because love covers a multitude of sins. Be hospitable to one another without complaint. As each one has received a special gift, employ it in serving one another as good stewards of the manifold grace of God."

The love shown by the men in my small group Bible study goes beyond the work parties. I know they will always be there to support me, build me up, and point me to the Lord. That is love.

The Addition

Once you have found a church family that takes their walk with the Lord seriously and truly lives out the commandment, "Love your neighbor as yourself," anything is possible. For example, the response to this Facebook post I made in May 2018 is unbelievable. Here's the post:

"When our circumstances seem unbearable and unchanging, I'm reminded today that while our circumstances may not be changing, at least not now, our perspective can change. The Lord keeps on bringing me back to this promise: 2 Corinthians 4:7-10 'But we have this treasure in earthen vessels, so that the surpassing greatness of the power will be of God and not from ourselves; we are afflicted in every way, but not crushed; perplexed, but not despairing; persecuted, but not forsaken; struck down, but not destroyed; always carrying about in the body the dying of Jesus, so that the life of Jesus also may be manifested in our body.'

"I'm always reminded in James 5:16 that 'The effective prayer of a righteous man can accomplish much.' So with that being said. Here are some prayer requests for my family. Michele and I are so grateful that Dan and Connie, Michele's parents, have been able to help us for the past year. They have been THE reason why I am still able to maintain a steady income to support my family. They take great care of the kids in my absence, they care for Michele, on some days when I get home from work, instead of resting, they shop for groceries when needed, they pick up the kids from school, the list goes on and on. They have been incredibly self-sacrificing and for that I am grateful. But as time goes on, not knowing what the future holds, my family of five and the two of them need our own space. Also, Conner is getting to the point where his own room would be good for him to have, instead of sharing with his two younger brothers. We have racked our brains trying to figure out what the best thing is we should do. Dan and Connie have given themselves to us for the indefinite future. They are currently looking for a house nearby, but with the rise of inflation over the past few years, that option doesn't look feasible. We are now seriously contemplating building an addition to our house for an "in-law suite." But that option, at the moment, doesn't look feasible either. I'm also reminded in Ephesians 3:20-21 that, 'Now to Him who is able to do far more abundantly beyond all that we ask or think, according to the power that works within us, to Him be the glory in the church and in Christ Jesus to all generations forever and ever. Amen.' Also, Philippians 4:19-20 tells us, 'And my God will supply all your needs according to His riches in glory in Christ Jesus. Now to our God and Father be glory forever and ever. Amen.'"

The result of that post was truly beyond anything I could have asked for or expected. I received a phone call from a fellow church member asking if I had time during the day to meet with him. I told him I could meet with him during my lunch break at work. When we got together, he said he and his wife were prepared to help. I wasn't sure what he meant at the time. He asked me for permission to take the lead with us. Permission was granted, of course.

To better explain what happened next, this is the story as told by my fellow brother in Christ, the one who took the lead in the project:

> "In June 2017, the Rezewski family experienced a traumatic change in their lives. Michele suffered a severe stroke from Moyamoya disease and was partially paralyzed as a result. Constant care for her became a necessity. Her husband, Brett, and her parents, Dan and Connie Conlon, became on-site care providers when she was able to come home. The next year proved to be a significant challenge for the family of five (Brett, Michele and their three boys Conner, Easton and Kaiden) and the parents. The four adults and three boys occupied a three-bedroom, 1700 square foot home while attempting to continue their lives with as much normalcy as possible. Brett maintained his employment with the VA and Dan his business as a travel agent, while Connie provided care for Michele as she labored to regain capabilities lost to the stroke. All of them experienced significant stress that they felt could be somewhat relieved with a better housing situation.

> "This is the story of how the Lord changed their housing situation by providing the Conlon's with a space of their own. On May 22, 2018, a Facebook posting by Brett explained the stresses and desire to improve their housing situation. Subsequently, a church member met with Brett and received permission to aid them by helping with an assessment of options to meet their needs. The Rezewskis and Conlons had already explored some options. That included the Conlons selling their home in Spokane, Washington and buying a dwelling of some sort near the Rezewskis. Due to a large difference in property values, that idea was discarded. Acquisition of an RV or trailer was also

considered, but HOA regulations wouldn't allow parking one on the property.

"In June 2018, further exploration of more options began. The sale of the Rezewskis home and purchase of a larger home nearer Southwest Bible Church (where they worshiped and had enrolled their kids in school) was considered. A church member analyzed the value and availability of suitable homes and found that option would require a much larger mortgage for the Rezewskis (on the order of $100,000). Another church member analyzed mortgage adjustments and other avenues for financing available to the family. It was determined that all those options would result in a huge increase in mortgage payments - increases that could limit the funds available to put toward Michele's rehabilitation.

"It became clear that funds from a source outside the family would be required for any solution. Funding options considered were a GoFundMe campaign, private/personal appeals, and a designated giving campaign within the Southwest Bible Church family. Subsequently, an allocation of funds from the church's Body Life Fund was approved by the Church Council.

"In July 2018, a member of the church with a long history as a General Contractor was asked to oversee construction of an addition to the Rezewski's house that would provide the Conlons with a separate living space. He accepted the challenge and a plan was drawn up to build a 300 square foot addition, including a separate bathroom, a kitchenette, and an open bedroom/living space. About that time, an invitation to participate in the construction of the addition was sent out to about 15 men of the church who were known to have backgrounds in construction. The response was nearly 100% positive. The Lord was truly faithful in providing this group as a base for the construction to come.

"On August 23, only three days after submittal, Washington County issued permits for the project. This was an answer to prayer as applications were sometimes taking three to four weeks and any delays would push the construction into the return of the rainy season. (Note: the Lord provided excellent weather during September with only two days of any significant rain.) On August 24, demolition of the existing brick fireplace (which was on the wall where the addition was to be attached) kicked off the project. A church member stubbed off an existing natural gas line for future use (a gas stove was installed in the existing family room at the end of the project to replace the original wood burning fireplace).

"The following week saw the excavation of the crawl space. Church members provided a small track hoe and the skilled operators to do that job. A church member provided the forms for the foundation and, with the help of another skilled member, set them up on the last day of August. The foundation was poured on the 4th of September, and we were out of the ground!

"The following three Saturdays, saw groups of six to eight men from the church build the post and beam support for the floor, frame up and sheet the exterior walls, put up the roof trusses, and sheet the roof. These groups of skilled and semi-skilled framers were all recruited from within the church by a member who expertly planned and guided them. Another church member provided a crane to lift the trusses (which were designed, pre-built, and donated by a local company) to the roof. The roofing material was donated by a local roofing company and installed by another one on September 24. Coordination of the different stages with workers and inspectors was critical for the project to proceed as quickly as possible. This was amazing progress on the project, since nearly all the work was being done by volunteers who were fitting in their time while holding regular day jobs. The outside contractors also bent over backwards to accommodate our needs at critical times. God's hand was evident in all of that.

"Interior walls and rough-in plumbing and electrical were completed by September 28 with the help of skilled professionals from the church and licensed contractors. By mid-October, the exterior siding, gutters and downspouts were installed - and painted by October 18. A crew put up drywall on October 19 and 20 and installed a skylight in the family room as well. While the crew worked on the skylight, a serious failure in an original truss member in another part of the house was discovered. Finding the problem just at that time was Providential! The repair entailed getting a 12-foot 2x6 into the attic, which would have required cutting a hole in the roof – which had already been done in order to install the skylight.

"In the last week of October, a professional drywall finisher (also a church member) applied many coats of mud and sanded the joints in preparation for the final stages of plumbing, electrical, and painting. A contractor applied texture to the ceiling and walls. In the first week of November, a church member laid the ceramic tile in the bathroom and a contractor installed the baseboards, window frames and interior doors, which were then painted by another contractor. At the same time, a couple church members built a cedar deck (with a ramp) over the existing concrete slab patio which greatly improved wheelchair access to the covered patio and backyard and a porch for the outside entry to the new addition.

"Finishing touches were accomplished in the last half of November. Carpet and a window covering (donated by a local business) were installed, as well as cabinets for the kitchenette. The cabinets were designed, built, and installed by another church member and accommodated a below-counter refrigerator, microwave, and small sink. Additional cabinetry for outdoor clothing and boot storage were also provided in the original laundry room. A natural gas stove (provided by a local business at less than cost) was installed in the family room by church members.

"On December 4, 2018, the Rezewski family hosted an open-house and celebration of God's provision of the addition to their home. Brett said the addition would stand as a memorial acknowledging the Lord's work in a significant event, much as the Israelites of old built memorials to remind future generations.

"Throughout the project, as church men were challenged to contribute their skills, time, equipment, and materials to meet the need, the response was overwhelming. The response was perfectly in line with Ephesians 2:10: 'For we are His workmanship, created in Christ Jesus for good works, which God prepared beforehand, that we should walk in them.' It was a beautiful thing to see it being worked out over and over! At least 36 men and women contributed labor to the effort, not including the laborers provided by contractors.

"Huge contributions of equipment, materials and laborers were also provided by local businesses during the project. Overall, it is estimated that 90 percent of all labor and about 70 percent of all materials were donated. As a result, the funds provided by Southwest Bible Church covered all other expenses. The objective of meeting the Rezewskis need for additional housing at no cost to them was accomplished. Praise the Lord!"

It should be emphasized that throughout this entire project, all the men who contributed their time came on nights and weekends. They all had jobs, families, and commitments to tend to, yet they all felt the call to offer their talents and time. To them, they were walking in obedience. That is love.

Michele's Love

This story would not be adequately told without sharing the kind of love Michele has. Michele is about as selfless of a person there is. She is constantly giving of her time, resources, and creative energy to make sure everyone feels loved. She even made the decision to give of herself in her death as she opted to be an organ donor.

Before Michele's stroke, she was the kind of person who was always there for people when they needed help. Even if people didn't ask for help, she would offer. Quite often, Michele would bring a meal to someone or watch their kids. She still loves to give gifts to people even now.

Michele wanted to make sure her heroes knew she was grateful for what they did. We went to the fire station to meet the paramedic who intubated her at our house. It was so good to shake his hand, and thank him for saving my wife. It turns out he retired from the military, so he and I were able to connect on that level as well. He was a brand-new paramedic. The first major call he responded to was Conner's call for Michele. He remembered in detail what had happened that night; he remembered the kids and the deputy jumping on the ball like a Pogo stick. He assured us that the kids were taken care of. He wanted us to know that they didn't see what was going on in the bedroom with Michele being intubated. He also thanked us for coming into the station because the workers rarely get to see the outcome of the people they care for.

We also wanted to pay a visit to Dr. Antezana. We scheduled an appointment, and the whole family went in to see him. It was great to meet under different circumstances. I told him I appreciated how he responded when I asked him if I should bring the kids in. He was impressed to see how well Michele was doing.

Michele with the paramedic who intubated her.

Even after the stroke, Michele has a desire to give. She puts treats outside our home for truck drivers when they deliver packages, especially around Christmas. She loves to bake Christmas cookies for others. Michele remembers the birthdays of friends and sends gifts to friends that have moved away. She is always thinking about how she can be a blessing, which is something I deeply love about her.

CHAPTER 9

Birmingham and Hope Heals Camp

Within a couple of weeks of the stroke, there were people praying for Michele all over the world. As the word got out about what happened to her, we started to hear about groups and organizations that were beneficial to check out. A friend of our family told us about a book called *Hope Heals*. It's about the story of Katherine and Jay Wolf. As stated on their website (www.hopeheals.com), "Katherine had suffered a massive brain stem stroke (in 2008) out of the blue, from the rupturing of an AVM, a rare congenital defect she didn't even know she had." According to her neurosurgeon, "it was the largest AVMs he has ever seen, in the worst location. She was not expected to live." But he took the case anyway. Maybe he had a glimmer of hope, like Dr. Antezana had with Michele.

I read the book to Michele while I visited her in the hospital. It was comforting to know that we weren't, and aren't, alone; that others have experienced similar trials and have overcome them. We learned that our story had many similarities to theirs: The verse I read while Michele underwent emergency brain surgery, Romans 8:18, was the same that Jay read to his supporters while they were waiting for his bride's surgery; Jay had a community of friends and family gathered at the hospital with him while Katherine was getting operated on after the stroke; Katherine was given a wooden structure in the form of a cross that she held in her hand to maintain its range of motion, and Michele was given the same thing without knowing the Wolf's story; It took both Michele and Katherine time to be able to talk again; Both Katherine and Michele had to find alternative ways to communicate, with Katherine using a device that spoke when she punched in words and Michele writing on a white board.

All According to God's Plan

One other similarity worth mentioning is how the Lord led both my family and theirs to a different part of the country to prepare for what was to come. Years before the AVM ruptured in Katherine's brain, they moved from Georgia to Los Angeles, California. They immediately got involved in a church and started building their community. They became the leaders of a young marrieds' group, even though they had just gotten married themselves. Jay "just happened" to be home during the 45-minute window in which Katherine had the stroke. She was taken to the UCLA medical center where her neurosurgeon worked, who just *happened* to be one of the best in the country.

Do you see a pattern? Everything happens for a reason. Who knows? If the Wolfs had never moved across the country, maybe Kathrerine's story would have been different. If we didn't move to where we did in Oregon, maybe Michele's story would have been different. Expert neurosurgeons were at both UCLA and the hospital in Oregon, they both took their respective cases, and they both were moved by *hope* for positive outcomes with their patients.

Michele's Revelation

As Michele and I were reading *Hope Heals*, Michele learned about a retreat called Hope Heals Camp. It's held every year in a small town just outside of Birmingham, Alabama. We did some research, fell in love with the idea of going, and applied, just the two of us. We felt we needed to get away and connect without the kids. That year, a lottery system determined who could go to camp. From the time we submitted our application to the time of selection, which was a few months, we prayed hard. Friends were praying. People in our church were praying. We felt like Hope Heals Camp would be a place where God would bring some emotional healing to our tattered hearts. After those few months of praying and waiting, an email finally came. *We were in*! We were going to Alabama! I sent a response email to the staff at Hope Heals telling them our story because I expected Katherine and Jay would relate with it. A few days later, Katherine herself responded, which was very exciting for us.

Shortly after, we learned that the Wolfs were scheduled to speak at a church close to our home. That was an opportunity we didn't want to miss, so, in May 2018, we drove the 40 minutes to Rolling Hills Community Church. Michele and I resonated with the presentation deeply. We remembered their story from what we read in their book, but seeing and hearing them talk about it in person

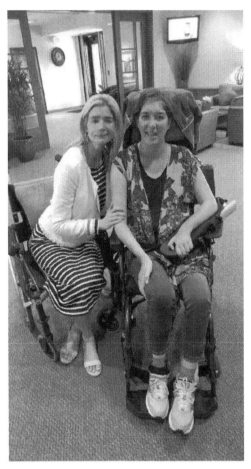

brought everything to life. Listening to them speak also gave us an increased sense of hope. Katherine and Jay were fun to listen to; they brought the quirks of their relationship into the presentation. They're just like any other married couple, even with their incident.

After the service, we waited in line to meet them as they were giving away copies of their book. When it was our turn, they immediately knew who we were. We could have talked with them the rest of the day, but we tried to keep it brief since there were others waiting. But, before we left, we made sure to take pictures. Meeting the Wolfs prior to Hope Heals Camp made it even more exciting for me and Michele to go. Katherine and Michele had connected as stroke survivors, and Jay and I had connected as husband caregivers. We weren't alone.

Leaving on a Jet Plane

Finally, the day to depart Portland had arrived. Hope Heals Camp, here we come! Traveling on a plane with a wheelchair is an adventure, but this was all part of our "new normal." We just rolled with each thing that came along (no pun intended). We had to be very selective about the itinerary and consider basic needs though. For example, the bathrooms on planes are barely big enough for someone who can walk in, let alone someone needing to fit a wheelchair. Because of that, we had to time each leg of our trip just right for Michele's comfort.

Walking around the airport itself was another ordeal, but Michele and I don't shy away from a good challenge. Michele pushed the big suitcase in front of her while I pushed her in the wheelchair. We hung another bag on the back of her wheelchair, and I had our carry-on on my back. I wish someone had taken a video of us as we maneuvered around the terminal.

At each gate, we had to speak with the attendant ahead of time to let them know we had a wheelchair.

As someone with a disability, Michele could board before everyone else, which was both good and not so good for us. It was helpful because we didn't have to battle everyone else finding their seats, but at the same time, it was bad because it meant longer waiting periods for Michele to have access to a bathroom. We had to wait for the workers to bring us a special wheelchair narrow enough for the aisles. Sometimes that took almost an extra hour after landing, which was hard on Michele. Too bad they don't make airplanes more accessible. Maybe that will change one day.

Change of Scenery

We arrived in Birmingham on a Saturday night. Stepping out of the airport, we immediately could tell we weren't in Oregon anymore. The climate in the Pacific Northwest is usually on the dryer side, with the temperature only flirting with triple digits on occasion during the summer. It's quite different in the Deep South; it felt like we were stepping into a sauna. Poor Michele had to grab onto my sticky, sweaty neck whenever she needed to be transferred. Nonetheless, we were determined to explore while we had the chance, and the first thing we wanted to experience there was church. So, even though we didn't get to our hotel until late, we attended a church called The Church at Brook Hills early the next morning.

The church had a beautiful campus with many handicap parking spots. The usual pastor didn't bring the sermon that day; instead, Herbie Newell brought the Word, and it was powerful. He is the president and executive director of an organization called Lifeline Children's Services, which helps families through the adoption journey and provides them with resources. He spoke about gospel-driven justice for the fatherless, the orphans, the needy, and for those in foster care. He said that if we could hear the testimonials of people who have stepped up to participate in the Lifeline movement, we would hear the heartache in their voices as they recalled the kids' difficult stories. He quoted Paul David Tripp in his sermon:

> "You are tempted to think that because you're God's child, your life should be easier, more predictable, and definitely more comfortable. But that's not what the Bible teaches. Instead, it reveals that struggles are part of God's plan for you. This means that if you're God's child, you must never allow yourself to think that the hard things you are now going through are failures of God's character, promises, power, or plan. You must not allow yourself to think that God has turned His back on you. You must not let yourself begin to buy into the possibility that God is not as trustworthy as your thought."

The Church at Brook Hills was formerly pastored by David Platt. If you haven't read his book, *Radical,* you need to. He has a huge heart for adopting and fostering children. At one point, he called the social services department in Birmingham and asked to know how many kids were in the system. Shortly after that phone call, every child in the system had a new place to call their home; the members of David's church had stepped up to take them all in. He left a legacy at The Church at Brook Hills.

Herbie's sermon had a profound impact on me. A couple of years before Michele's stroke, I had approached her with the idea of adopting a child. I believe God placed that desire on my heart back then and has allowed it to remain to this day. At the time, Michele wasn't sure about the idea, so I prayed a very specific prayer to the God who cares about the vulnerable, the stranger, the orphan, the destitute, and the fatherless. I prayed, "Lord, if we are supposed to adopt a child, let Michele's heart align with mine." Fast-forward to about a year after the stroke. Michele and I were alone in the car when, out of the blue, she said that she had been thinking about adopting a child. Wait, what? Really? I told her about my prayer a couple of years prior. It excited me to know that it was answered. But things were different then. We discussed the idea further; I told her that I work full-time outside the home, and we need help from her parents to take care of her and the kids we already have. How can we possibly take in another child? I must remember though that the God we serve is the same One who created the heavens, the universe, and everything in it. Surely, He will provide a way if that's what He wants us to do. I believe that if He planted that dream in our hearts, He will carry it out in His time.

Scavenger Hunt and a Thunderstorm

There should totally be a sixth love language, and Michele says it should be treats. She loves treats. Who doesn't, though? Michele found her happy place at Steel City Pops and Cookie Fix. Steel City Pops has arguably the most delicious gourmet popsicles on the planet. On a hot day like it was, those pops hit the spot. As far as Cookie Fix goes, I don't think I've ever had a cookie as good as what I had there. We bought some for Katherine, Jay, and their staff, and somehow managed to not eat them along the way.

While we were in Birmingham, we wanted to do some sightseeing. The history there is amazing. We went to the Sixteenth Street Baptist Church, where Martin Luther King Jr. preached. We read how it was bombed on September 15, 1963, killing four young girls. We went to Kelly Ingram Park, where Michele and I took in as much as we could from the emotional sculptures. We learned about the water cannons that were used to hammer the "child crusaders", the vicious dogs unleashed on them, and the throwing of those children in jail. It was all a sobering experience, especially when we realized we were on the same path the protesters walked during the Civil Rights Movement. We spent a good amount of time immersing ourselves in the history and took several pictures.

Before we left the downtown area, Michele remembered a picture of an "Alabama" sign she saw on Pinterest, and she was determined to find it. She eventually spotted it from the car as we drove around, and I parked in the first vacant spot I could find, which wasn't very close by. I left the car on foot to find it by myself because I thought that would be easier than going together. Michele had a vague idea of where the sign was and described it to me before I left. After a bit of walking, I found the sign and took a picture. Then the storm hit. I wasn't used to thunderstorms since we have so few of them in Oregon, and the ones we do have are nothing like the storms they have there. I tried to sprint toward the car, but quickly encountered a problem; I forgot where the car was. I can't remember how long it took to actually find the car again, but it felt like an eternity. Just picture me, a lonely tourist, scrambling all over the downtown area in the pouring rain. Oh, and don't forget the occasional burst of lightning. That was something else. I was thankful I wasn't struck.

Last Stop: Hope Heals Camp

With our excitement sky-high, yet still not knowing what to expect, we made our way to Nauvoo, Alabama, where Camp McDowell, home to Hope Heals Camp, is located. As we made our last turn onto the property, there were signs posted on both sides of the road welcoming us. We were also greeted by one of the volunteers. They are the lifeblood of the camp. We were asked if we wanted a loud intro or a quiet one. Because we were already amped, we enthusiastically opted for the loud intro. Driving a little further, we realized we were in a very special place. The volunteers lined both

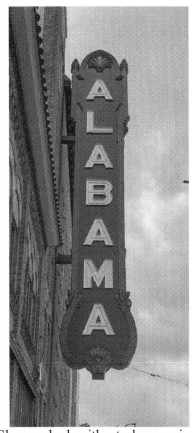

sides of the street, hootin' and hollerin' as we drove towards the Welcome Center. One of the volunteers had a sign with Michele's name on it. That was Amy, Michele's Compassionate Companion (CC). Every camper who has a disability or a child eight and under is paired with a CC. Their job is to make sure the camper has the time of their life. Essentially, they become your best friend. They make sure their camper gets to all the activities they want, and they provide a much-needed respite for the family and the caregivers. Amy was a physical therapist. How fitting for Michele to be with a PT!

She worked with stroke survivors and was well-familiar with our struggles. She was incredibly nice to us and over-delivered on every level. Her servant's heart ensured we were well taken care of.

Hope Heals Camp was the first time since the stroke where Michele and I felt like people "get it." We knew that people back home loved and cared for us. We knew that they were there to help when we needed it and to listen when we needed an ear. Lord knows, they proved that. But they don't know what it was like to "walk in

127

our shoes." The people at Hope Heals Camp do. They could empathize with us in ways that others couldn't, which was huge. Michele and I both experienced emotional healing that we desperately needed.

At Hope Heals Camp, there was a little boy, we'll call him "Tim", running around with two prosthetic legs. He was so happy to be there and to play with the other kids. Michele and I learned about his story. Tragically, his dad didn't realize Tim was behind him when he went into reverse on their riding lawn mower. Praise the Lord, Tim survived. We met his parents, who are amazing people with a passionate heart for Jesus. Then, we met another incredibly inspiring man who also had a prosthetic leg. He became someone that Tim looked up to; someone that understood exactly what he will go through for the rest of his life. It was so neat to see the other man take Tim under his wing.

It didn't take long at all to make more connections with people. Camp McDowell has many cabins spread out over the campus, each with a covered porch and chairs for people to sit and talk. We spent time on the porches sharing our story, as well as listening to others'. We all had our own tunnel, which made it very easy to start conversations. It felt so natural to dive deep into each other's lives. I found the question, "What's your story?" was a very effective icebreaker.

Some stories were heartbreaking. Two families there had a child with an extremely rare genetic defect that greatly limited their mobility from birth. In fact, when they were at camp, there were only eight known cases of the genetic mutation, yet they were able to meet and connect. I can't imagine how lonely they must have felt prior to that, thinking that they were all alone in their struggle. Those relationships were clearly ordained by the Lord.

People with all sorts of special needs found themselves at camp, including those with Down Syndrome, Cerebral Palsy, ASD, and many others. There were several adults who were stroke survivors. Michele and I had an instant connection with them. Still other adults endured different forms of traumatic brain injury. As people shared their stories, we learned that a lot of them felt alone and misunderstood—until they arrived at camp. Many tears were shed as people realized they had found a community that finally understood. It didn't matter what they struggled with at home; they found instant connection while at camp. The labels placed on them by society didn't matter while they were there. This was especially evident during the talent show, which I'll talk about later.

Gathering around the table in front of a delicious meal is a great way to bond with people. Katherine writes about the significance of food in their book, *Hope Heals.* She explains how it's not just about food consumption; "Eating is life. It's what humans do. It's how they socialize." In their first book, Katherine talks about the struggle she had after her stroke when she couldn't eat. She writes about how devastated she was after not passing her ninth swallow study. She had felt deep in her heart that it was part of God's plan for her to pass the study, so she could eat Thanksgiving dinner with her family that year, but during the Thanksgiving gathering, a thought snuck into Katherine's head as she watched her three sister-in-laws playing with her son. She couldn't eat, she couldn't walk, and she couldn't take care of her son. "Surely, this is not right. This is a mistake." Then she writes, "And before that thought could even fully land, I had this moment of… 'Katherine, are you crazy? I know better than you know. I'm God, and you're not. I don't make mistakes. There is a purpose in all of this. Just wait; you'll see!'"

If it wasn't for her stroke, Hope Heals Camp wouldn't exist.

The staff at the camp made sure each mealtime was meaningful. People were given the opportunity to be the hands and feet of Jesus, to serve those who needed to be served. The CCs were tasked with bringing food to the table and then bringing the empty baskets back, which would then be filled up again. They worked like a well-oiled machine. Michele and I were able to connect with a lot of other people around the table. More stories were shared and more relationships forged.

We loved gathering in the chapel for praise and worship. The Wolfs invited Sandra McCracken to sing each day, and hearing her was truly a blessing to our souls. At every service, you could feel the Lord's presence. You could feel His blessing on the work that was being done there. After times of worship in which hands were raised and tears fell, our hearts were prepared to hear the message. Everyone in that room needed healing of some sort. We were ready. God was with us. He always is.

When the Wolfs Speak, People Listen

Katherine and Jay brought the teaching that year, and when they speak, people listen. They listen because the Wolfs come from a place of suffering. They've been there and have been refined by their pain. The Wolfs spoke on remembering the trauma of disability; about the importance of being part of a community that builds you up. Furthermore, they spoke about being part of something bigger than yourself. They talked about the brokenness that brings healing.

That statement seems paradoxical, doesn't it? How can brokenness bring healing? Sometimes we don't leave room in our lives for the One who can heal. He uses our brokenness to bring us close to Him. Essentially, He becomes our light while we feel trapped in our tunnel.

The Wolfs also shared about the importance of finding Ebenezers, which, as put by Merriam-Webster's dictionary, is "a commemoration of divine assistance." One of the Ebenezers they use is an anchor. Jay describes in *Suffer Strong,* their second book, that anchors are an image that reminds them of Hebrews 6:19, which reads, "We have this hope as an anchor for the soul, a hope both sure and steadfast and one which enters within the veil." He says, "Quite appropriately, an anchor has a cross embedded in its shape."

Small Groups Divinely Prepared for Us

After the Wolfs spoke, everyone broke off into small groups. There weren't any assigned groups that year, but amazingly, our group included young adults who had overcome strokes or other traumatic brain injuries. There was one couple in particular that we formed a unique bond with—Susan and Patrick. We have a lot in common. Patrick is retired from the US Air Force. I served in the same branch for eight years. Susan is a caregiver and spouse, like me. Patrick suffered a massive stroke, like Michele. His stroke occurred in 2015, two years before Michele's. It helped to talk with people who had gone through similar things before us. They offered encouragement, wisdom and inspired us to keep going. It's been encouraging to see Patrick's progress to this day. His stroke happened on the left side of his brain, which severely impacted his speech. When we saw him at Hope Heals Camp in 2018, he had a cane to help with his balance. Now, he can walk some distances without it.

The Fun Continues

A men's-only field trip was scheduled off campus. We carpooled to Jim'N Nick's Bar-B-Q. That's where I learned what Southern food is all about. What I loved most about that time was the opportunity I had to fellowship with people I hadn't met yet. The time spent there was more focused on each other since we didn't have any distractions. Besides the good food, that is.

While the men were eating and connecting, the women were getting spoiled. Hope Heals Camp offered a rejuvenating experience by treating the ladies to Spa Day. Hairstylists came in to turn all the ladies into southern belles. I remember Michele telling me they used tons of hairspray. Each of the ladies were also given a gift bag with jewelry and other goodies to take home.

As Hope Heals Camp was wrapping up, it was time for the much-anticipated talent show, with a dance party to follow. Michele and I had heard many of the campers' stories by now. We talked with them, hugged them, and cried with them. Now, it was their time to shine. The talent show at Hope Heals Camp was probably one of the most touching events I've ever experienced. I'll bet Michele would agree with me. Some of the kids who entered the talent show could barely move because of their disability, but they still found the courage to perform without the fear of judgment. One of those kids showed off their talent by beating a drum. Every time he beat that drum, the audience erupted with applause as if it was the best thing they'd ever seen. He was loved just as he was.

That display of love remained during the whole talent show. As Tim played the guitar, the audience erupted. A boy with CP sang, "God, You're so good, You're so good to me," and the audience erupted. We even had a girl show off her martial arts skills. Once again, the audience erupted. It was so fun watching all the kids on stage, without a care in the world; likewise, for the adults.

After the talent show, it was time for the grand finale: the dance party. This was huge for me and Michele. We had gone through so much that year. What Michele endured physically was too much to bear. What I went through emotionally was a lot to bear as well. But Michele had come so far in her recovery, far exceeding the expectations of most doctors. We celebrated that night. I felt like it wasn't a real dance party unless I danced with my wife, so I stood her up out of that wheelchair, and we danced! That's when one of my favorite pictures of us was taken.

As I wrote this book, I was often inspired by looking at the hundreds of pictures taken along the way. For instance, I have a video of Michele dancing in her wheelchair during that party that brings a huge smile to my face and tears at the same time. You can tell she is happy. Her hand is raised in the air (I'm sure both hands would have been if she were able to raise the other one) and a beaming smile is on her face. Despite what she went through, she was enjoying the moment.

God allowed our tanks to be filled while at camp, which left us on an emotional high. However, it was soon time to go home and re-enter reality. The adjustment was hard. Both of us even sunk into a bit of a depression, which is very unusual for us. We longed to still be plugged in to that community. Fortunately, we remain connected to some wonderful people from camp, and we did eventually settle into our normal routine at home again.

CHAPTER 10

A Caregiver's Perspective

I think it's important to remember that the person who endures an affliction isn't the only one who suffers; the family suffers too. Yet so much focus, for obvious reasons, is placed on the one who physically endures the hardship. Oftentimes, the one who experienced the injury or illness isn't aware of what happened to them, but the family is. They're the ones who are forced to make the hard decisions. For example, my wife couldn't help me make the decision between keeping our baby alive or not. Granted, I sought wise counsel. But if I didn't have that to lean on, what would I have done? What if somebody is faced with that decision who doesn't know the Lord or have His people to lead them? How can they ever find peace, knowing their signature gave the approval to abort their child? God knew what I needed to help me with this very difficult decision. His hand is in every intricate detail. Everything that happened in the past and everything that will happen in the future is by His design.

When people have a stroke, a car accident, or any joint replacement surgery, there's usually the opportunity for that person to participate in some form of physical or occupational therapy. Depending on the severity of the injury, that therapy may be prescribed by a doctor to last for days, months, or even years in some cases. That therapy is designed to help the patient recover as many losses as they can. Yes, there is immediate help for the family after tragedy strikes and life changes in an instant; a chaplain is usually on scene to help with any needs, if they arise, but quite often, the help for the family stops there. This could be a choice that the loved one makes because they feel they don't need the help, or it could be the result of inadequate opportunities for the continuation of therapy.

There remains a stigma around counseling. So often, we believe it's a sign of weakness to seek help. We don't want to bother anyone with our problems. We believe that God will help us get through the hardest times. Of course, that is true. God strengthens those who are weak. But the Bible does instruct us to not do it alone. Whether it's in the form of a trustworthy friend or a licensed therapist, don't try and do it alone. Here are some verses from the Bible to back up this argument:

- "Therefore encourage one another and build up one another, just as you also are doing," (1 Thessalonians 5:11).
- "Let us hold fast the confession of our hope without wavering, for He who promised is faithful; and let us consider how to stimulate one another to love and good deeds, not forsaking our own assembling together; and all

the more as you see the day drawing near,"
(Hebrews 10:23-25).

- "Two are better than one because they have a good return for their labor. For if either of them falls, the one who will lift up his companion. But woe to the one who falls when there is not another to lift him up. Furthermore, if two lie down together they keep warm, but how can one be warm alone? And if one can overpower him who is alone, two can resist him. A cord of three strands is not quickly torn apart," (Ecclesiastes 4:9-12).

- "Iron sharpens iron, so one man sharpens another," (Proverbs 27:17).

While Michele was in the OR for the initial brain surgery, multiple people told me that I needed to take care of myself. They used the "mask on an airplane" analogy. They said, "Before you put the mask on others, you should put it on yourself." That makes sense, but it's not easy to do. A caregiver constantly has the mindset of helping the person they are caring for, but if the caregiver isn't taking care of themselves, sooner or later they won't be able to care for either one of them.

Early on, I wasn't taking as good of care of myself as I should have, especially mentally. I had to return to work less than a week after her stroke. I was not okay. In fact, I was angry. People would come in for X-rays with a sore finger. Meanwhile, my wife is fighting for her life in the hospital. I'd put on a cheery face for the patient; I smiled and tried to be positive while they were there.

However, I grew bitter as soon as they left. I sent a text out to my men's group telling them how I was doing and asking for prayer. My perspective immediately changed when the next patient came in. He asked me if I'd heard about the collision between the USS Fitzgerald – a US Navy Destroyer – and the MV ACX Crystal – a Philippine flagged container ship. Seven US Sailors died in that collision. As soon as he told me that, a wave of gratitude washed over me. Despite all the hardships we had endured, Michele was still alive. Seven families found out that day that they weren't whole anymore. I believe God brought that person in to help me get off the pity train. That train would've taken me to the pit of despair. Nothing good happens there.

Over the past three and a half years, I've learned what I need in order to show up better for my wife and kids. I learned how to put my mask on first before anyone else. I make sure I take care of my needs, which requires me to be the first to rise in the morning. I've developed a routine that sets my day up well. It includes daily time in the Bible, exercise, and reading a good book. If I don't have my "me time", my tank remains empty, and I may not be as loving towards my wife and kids.

One other facet about being a caregiver I want to touch on is the desire to be appreciated. Caregivers work hard to take care of the person they're caring for, especially if it involves family. We take on the role of caregiver without the expectation to be appreciated, but having the recognition sure helps.

When we don't feel appreciated as caregivers, we can always read what Jesus says in Matthew 6:4; "Your Father who sees in secret will reward you." John Piper, from the Ask Pastor John Podcast, emphasizes this verse in one of his sermons. He says, "It's a God issue. It's a God issue. It's a God issue. It's a God issue. That's the way you'll survive when every effort of love disappears in a black hole. It's a God issue that will keep you smiling. It's a God issue that will keep you hopeful and happy and resourceful and flowing and flowing and flowing till the day you die, when nobody says, 'Thank you.' It's a God issue. You can bring more glory to your God by pressing on, in thankless love, than you can by any other means." What can I say after that besides amen!

I know Michele's parents can attest to this. They do many things for us every day, and probably only a fraction of the things they do gets recognized. Service to them comes as naturally as breathing. They have served our family now for over three years. They left their familiar, comfortable lives in Spokane, Washington, and sold their house. Dan's travel agency business took a hit, especially during the COVID-19 pandemic. They were on the verge of being able to retire. But the Lord had other plans for them, and they obeyed. When I think of them and how they abandoned the lives they knew, I'm reminded of how the twelve disciples responded to Jesus when He said, "Come with Me." Without question, they left their familiar lives and followed Jesus. Same with Michele's parents. They didn't ask if we needed their help; they just saw a need and responded.

One of the hardest things for me as a caregiver and husband is finding the balance between the two. Both require time, but the tasks fall into different categories of time. Michele wants to spend time with me where I'm not taking care of her. She wants time with me when I remove the "caregiver hat." This is a struggle because I only have a few hours in the evening when I get home from work, and there's always a lot to do. Also, don't forget, we have three boys. They are excited to see me when I get home. They want me to see this Lego creation, or that painting, or tell me about what they did in Minecraft, or anything else from that day. I'm glad to see or hear what they have for me, but admittedly, it can get overwhelming at times.

Why Did This Happen?

One of the difficulties I've had to navigate since Michele's stroke is trying to answer a question that many have when experiencing hardships. Michele would ask me, "What did I do that caused God to allow this to happen to me?" When people have this question, they may think God is a judge with a gavel, and He can't wait to slam it down as He pronounces the sentence.

I asked God for wisdom to respond. The answer I received is found in John 9:1-3:

> "As He passed by, He saw a man blind from birth. And His disciples asked Him, 'Rabbi (which means teacher), who sinned, this man or his parents, that he would be born blind?' Jesus answered, 'It was neither that this man sinned, nor his parents; but it was so that the works of God might be displayed in him.'"

The rest of the chapter describes how the man gained his sight.

Jesus "spat on the ground and made clay of the spittle, and applied the clay to his eyes," (John 9:6). Then, Jesus gave specific instructions to the man, and he followed them. The man was then able to see for the first time in his life. That's when the controversy started. People were questioning if the man was even blind to begin with, to which the man's parents testified he was always blind. Some people said, "This man (Jesus) is not from God, because He does not keep the Sabbath," (John 9:16). The Pharisees were relentless in questioning the man who was blind. Finally, he responded in verse 30, saying, "Well, here is an amazing thing, that you do not know where He is from, and yet He opened my eyes."

My answer to Michele's question is this: "God allowed you to have your stroke so that His power will be evident in your life and in ours." Throughout this book, you have read how God's power has been evident in our story. I can't imagine what Michele has been through. We wouldn't have a story like this to tell if she hadn't suffered. My heart truly goes out to her. She is the most courageous woman I've ever met. She is the reason why I push so hard. She and the kids are my "why." What also keeps me going is the fact that God's not done with us. Our story is still being written. I'm so excited to see what He has in store for us. Lord willing, we'll be able to see the purpose of all the suffering we've endured because of the stroke, but we may never fully know until we are at His side; until we see Him as He is, face to face. I can only imagine. Oh, how we long to hear those words from Him, "Well done, good and faithful servant," (Matthew 25:21).

Hope [UN]deferred

CHAPTER 11

A Glimpse of Light

Every tunnel has a beginning and an end. Likewise, every trial has a beginning and an end. It's dark while you are in the tunnel, but as you keep going, you eventually start seeing a glimpse of light. Before your eyes adjust to the light, you may find yourself squinting. Keep pressing on. As you keep going, the light will become more apparent.

That describes how our lives have been since the stroke. While there doesn't appear to be a light at the end of our tunnel, we've had to look at our circumstances from a different perspective. We've seen beauty rise from our ashes. For example, my sister, Lauren, surrendered her life to Christ, which I couldn't be happier about. She said in a text, "You guys had a major influence on me. Just watching you and how strong your faith was when she had her stroke really got me thinking that I was missing something in my life. The prayers for her and the milestones she was making and proving the doctors wrong was definitely God's work."

Others have told us that our story has inspired them to press on when trials appear too much to bear. This is both humbling and exciting. It's humbling for the fact that people see us and what we've been through, and it helps them get through their own difficulties. It's exciting because we know God is in control, and He's not done writing out our story.

The Fight Continues

When Michele was lying unconscious right after the stroke, I went up to her and whispered, "Michele, you need to fight for us." She heard me, and she fought. Hard! At the time of writing this, five years have passed since the stroke, and the fight still continues. Every day is a battle as she remembers the things she lost. She doesn't feel like she can be the mom she once was. She's not able to get the boys up and get them ready for school like she used to. She's not able to stand on her own and do the dishes or cook. She's only able to use her right arm. So, yes, the fight continues. But we hold on to the hope that everything we have been through and are going through has a purpose. No matter what happened or what will happen, the suffering is not, and will never be, wasted. God promises that it's all meant for good. Our hope doesn't need to be deferred, as long as it's grounded in Christ. Neither does yours.

We have assurance knowing that our life is in His hands. Even in death. Do you agree that death is the worst thing that can possibly happen to your mortal body? He knows the exact minute, the exact second of your last breath. Because of that, why worry about it? God has you in the palm of His hand. So, no matter what you are going through right now, no matter how serious it is, no matter how devastated you are, know that it's not for nothing. God is there for you. He is with you. With that assurance, continue the fight. Continue pressing on through your own tunnel. Look for those glimpses of light.

Epilogue

As I mentioned in the introduction, here are the verses that make up the Romans Road. These verses can be used to "walk" towards a saving relationship with Jesus.

1. Romans 1:20-21: "For since the creation of the world, His invisible attributes, His eternal power and divine nature, have been clearly seen, being understood through what has been made, so that they are without excuse. For even though they knew God, they did not honor Him as God or give thanks, but they became futile in their speculations, and their foolish heart was darkened."
2. Romans 3:10: "...as it is written, 'There is none righteous, not even one.'"
3. Romans 3:23: "...for all have sinned and fall short of the glory of God..."
4. Romans 6:23: "For the wages of sin is death, but the free gift of God is eternal life in Christ Jesus our Lord."
5. Romans 5:8: "But God demonstrates His own love toward us, in that while we were yet sinners, Christ died for us."

6. Romans 10:9-10: "…that if you confess with your mouth Jesus as Lord, and believe in your heart that God raised Him from the dead, you will be saved; for with the heart a person believes, resulting in righteousness, and with the mouth he confesses, resulting in salvation."
7. Romans 10:13: "…for 'Whoever will call on the name of the Lord will be saved.'"

These verses were used on me while I was in the military. I was stationed at Keesler Air Force Base in Biloxi, Mississippi for a time. A friend in my unit invited me to attend his church, Grace Independent Baptist Church. It was there that I responded to an "altar call." After the service, it was a former Marine who led me down the Romans Road. The next Sunday, I was baptized. Praise the Lord!

Hope remains the reason why we push on. Hope in God's plan for us. Hope that our lives would mean something; that our suffering would mean something. If even one person who reads this book has found strength to keep going, then the purpose for writing has been met.

The metaphor of a light at the end of a tunnel I've used to describe the trial we face reminds me of the poem *Footprints in the Sand* (author unknown):

> One night a man had a dream. He dreamed
> he was walking along the beach with the LORD.

Across the sky flashed scenes from his
life. For each scene he noticed two sets of
footprints in the sand: one belonging to
him, and the other to the LORD.

When the last scene of his life flashed before
him, he looked back at the footprints in the sand.

He noticed that many times along the path of
his life there was only one set of footprints.

He also noticed that it happened at the
very lowest and saddest times in his life.

This really bothered him and he
questioned the LORD about it:

"LORD, you said that once I decided to
follow you, you'd walk with me all the way.
But I have noticed that during the
most troublesome times in my life,
there is only one set of footprints.
I don't understand why when
I needed you most you would leave me."

The LORD replied:

"My son, my precious child,
I love you and I would never leave you.
During your times of trial and suffering,
when you see only one set of footprints,
it was then that I carried you."

Truly, the Lord has carried us through all our pain. He carried us when Jacob died. He carried us the day Michele had the stroke. He carried us through the pain of letting go of our baby. And there is no doubt, He'll carry us through whatever lies ahead. So, we press on.

Another detail I haven't mentioned yet is the shirt Michele wore the day everything changed. It said, "Hope Changes Everything." How fitting for her to wear that shirt, not knowing what was going to happen that day. That detail was also part of His plan. His hand has been, and will be, interwoven into every intricate detail.

This is the shirt that Michele had worn the night of the stroke.

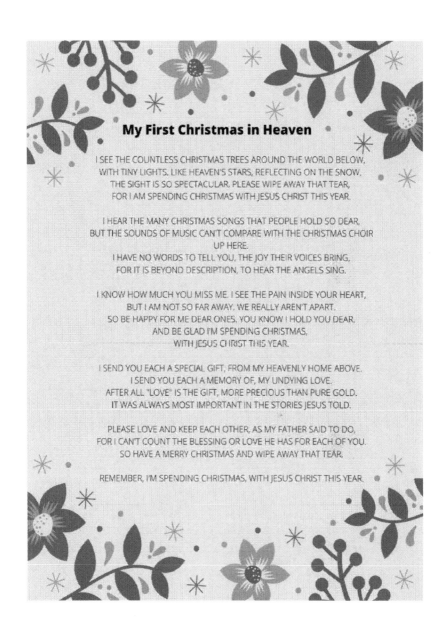

My First Christmas in Heaven

I SEE THE COUNTLESS CHRISTMAS TREES AROUND THE WORLD BELOW,
WITH TINY LIGHTS, LIKE HEAVEN'S STARS, REFLECTING ON THE SNOW.
THE SIGHT IS SO SPECTACULAR, PLEASE WIPE AWAY THAT TEAR,
FOR I AM SPENDING CHRISTMAS WITH JESUS CHRIST THIS YEAR.

I HEAR THE MANY CHRISTMAS SONGS THAT PEOPLE HOLD SO DEAR,
BUT THE SOUNDS OF MUSIC CAN'T COMPARE WITH THE CHRISTMAS CHOIR
UP HERE.
I HAVE NO WORDS TO TELL YOU, THE JOY THEIR VOICES BRING,
FOR IT IS BEYOND DESCRIPTION, TO HEAR THE ANGELS SING.

I KNOW HOW MUCH YOU MISS ME. I SEE THE PAIN INSIDE YOUR HEART,
BUT I AM NOT SO FAR AWAY. WE REALLY AREN'T APART.
SO BE HAPPY FOR ME DEAR ONES, YOU KNOW I HOLD YOU DEAR,
AND BE GLAD I'M SPENDING CHRISTMAS,
WITH JESUS CHRIST THIS YEAR.

I SEND YOU EACH A SPECIAL GIFT, FROM MY HEAVENLY HOME ABOVE.
I SEND YOU EACH A MEMORY OF, MY UNDYING LOVE.
AFTER ALL "LOVE" IS THE GIFT, MORE PRECIOUS THAN PURE GOLD.
IT WAS ALWAYS MOST IMPORTANT IN THE STORIES JESUS TOLD.

PLEASE LOVE AND KEEP EACH OTHER, AS MY FATHER SAID TO DO,
FOR I CAN'T COUNT THE BLESSING OR LOVE HE HAS FOR EACH OF YOU.
SO HAVE A MERRY CHRISTMAS AND WIPE AWAY THAT TEAR,

REMEMBER, I'M SPENDING CHRISTMAS, WITH JESUS CHRIST THIS YEAR.

—Author Unknown

Made in United States
Troutdale, OR
07/17/2023

11317211R00093